TALKING ABOUT THE WAR

Talking about the War . . .

ANNE VALERY

LARGE PRINT
Oxford, England

First published in Great Britain 1991
by Michael Joseph Ltd, part of the Penguin Group of Companies

Published in Large Print 1992 by Clio Press,
55 St. Thomas' Street, Oxford OX1 1JG,
by arrangement with Michael Joseph Ltd

Photograph in Introduction supplied
by courtesy of Paul Popper Ltd

British Library Cataloguing in Publication Data
Valery, Anne
 Talking About the War: 1939–45 – A Personal
 View of the War in Britain – New ed
 I. Title
 941.084092

ISBN 1-85695-010-7

Printed and bound by Hartnolls Ltd, Bodmin, Cornwall
Cover designed by CGS Studios Ltd, Cheltenham

To all those who resist censorship

CONTENTS

LIST OF ABBREVIATIONS

AFS	Auxiliary Fire Service
ARP	Air Raid Precautions
ATS	Auxiliary Territorial Service (Women)
CD	Civil Defence
ENSA	Entertainments National Service Association
HD	Heavy Duty Rescue
LD	Light Duty Rescue
HG	Home Guard
MOF	Ministry of Food
MOI	Ministry of Information
NFS	National Fire Service
WAAF	Women's Auxiliary Air Force
WRNS	Women's Royal Naval Service
WVS	Women's Voluntary Service
AWOL	Absent Without Leave

PREFACE

I am not an historian, and this is not a potted history of the Second World War, though there are the basic facts of some of its facets. However, what I enjoy is comment, and my only justification for writing this book is that I *am* a writer, that I lived through the war both as a child and an adult, and that it made me opinionated.

It is this that I hope will give the reader an occasional new slant on a well-trodden subject, so that even if you disagree with what I say, you won't think "Yet another bloody book about the war".

Anne Valery
1990

INTRODUCTION

Once upon a time there were three wise men who had such a regard for truth that when the claws of Fascism stretched towards Eastern Europe, they set out for the foggy streets of London. It was the 1930s, and the men were Tom Blau, Stefan Lorant and Paul Popper, three refugees who would help to change the very face and content of our magazines. Tom founded the Camera Press; Stefan became editor of the magazines *Illustrated, Lilliput*, and *Picture Post*; while Paul, after a distinguished career as a photographer, opened a picture agency off Fleet Street.

Despite the bombing, the re-building fervour of the fifties and sixties and the greed of contemporary developers, Bride Lane still winds its narrow course between a hotch-potch of buildings and the brooding wall of St Bride's Church: a dark and secret sanctuary where Paul Popper set up shop on the top floor of Number 24. Miraculously, the warren of his offices still survives: a glorious jumble of passages, partitions and rooms that spill over with desks and shelves and boxes and filing cabinets that can barely contain the thousands upon thousands of photographs; a time capsule of how we were, lovingly housed by a staff that has a proper regard for history.

It was history that I was seeking when I entered the crammed fastness of the main office, for I'd been asked to write the text accompanying a collection of colour photographs commissioned for the wartime editions of *Illustrated*. When I saw them I was dazzled. They were as fresh and immediate as any photograph taken today, and I might have stopped there, except that researchers by their very nature are insatiable; and so, like the files around me, I spilled over into the black-and-whites, and the proof copies of the magazine itself. What made me ask if there were any censored photographs, I'll never know, but I did ask, and was rewarded by a treasure trove that had lain unseen for almost half a century: a car listing in a sea of rubble; a home sliced by blast, like a doll's house whose front had swung open; and, most chilling of all, a playground humped with the molehills of dead children. It was all there, the bottom line of war.

And there was something else: a sly and surreal levity that sometimes was all that stood between an embattled people and desolation.

To me this photograph says it all. A tatty but unbowed Union Jack; our love of wordplay in the combined statement and expletive of "BLAST"; the fashion model ravaged of all save her tipsy dignity; the girl's sad contemplation of a ruined dress costing many coupons, while behind her a man savours the unlikely position of a pair of legs. But wait. Look again. A severed hand and arm point to the hint of a bracelet around the model's ankle. Is she perhaps a tart, for that was the sign of office when the poodle was discarded because of the bombing? And, if so, what is her companion — the owner of the legs — up to? Could it be possible that the placard is masking an American GI or a Polish airman, or indeed any other of the many Allies under whose weight, it was said, both the country and its womanhood were sinking? More than likely, considering that a loosening of moral fibre and the dogs of war have always gone hand in hand, while the ubiquitous cry of "Don't you know there's a war on?" justified almost anything.

It was "Don't you know there's a war on?" that explained month-old letters, the non-arrival of all forms of transport, and indeed any other delay or loss, for there were few norms except the will to survive and to make the best of things. And we did. Which is why so many look back on the war and smile, for there was a warmth and a humour that would stun the youth of today; and if we were also tough and raunchy, that was fine too, for it has stood us in good stead in the cold and increasingly heartless world of today.

So long live nostalgia, and let us return to the distant past so as to set the scene.

The child clutches a penny, running across the cobbles

to the man balancing a tray on his head. "Muffins, lovely fresh muffins," he shouts, ringing his bell as he sidesteps a trail of horse dung that will be shovelled up for the greater glory of someone's garden. Later, with the sweet smell of the muffin warm on her fingers, the child stares down from a window at a chair-mender working under the gas lamp with his loops of creamy cane; at the knife-grinder's boot pumping the pedal that turns the whetstone that sharpens the knife, his horny thumb eager to test the blade that will cut a floating feather. At the rattle of a chain, the child turns and sees a tiny monkey in a fez, running the length of his tether on a barrel organ which its owner is dragging towards home.

This is not a description of nineteenth-century Britain, but of a street in London during the 1930s. To be precise: the child is me, and the time is just four years short of a war that was to be the watershed between life as it is lived today, and the last remnants of Victorian Britain. It is a past that was so different, that it makes those of us who were alive then feel like ghosts in our own lifetime.

Imagine if you can a world without the fear of radiation, where the seas were safe for fish, and the skies empty of the scream of jets; a world where farming continued in its time-honoured way, unpolluted by a blanket of chemicals, and in a countryside of high hedges enclosing a patchwork of fields, meadows, woods and seemingly lost villages watered by wells. A place of barn owls, badgers, butterflies, field mice and glow worms; of horse-drawn ploughs, haystacks, village ponds and blessed silence.

Then, there were far fewer cars in the cities, four

postal deliveries a day, attentive shop assistants, and civic centres that were monuments of local pride allied to Victorian money. Above all, imagine if you can a seemingly predictable future in which most of the women stayed at home, and where sons followed their fathers and grandfathers into the same trade in the same firm. An idyllic time, you might think, except that it was underpinned by the riches and loot from the Colonies, and chose to ignore the misery of its poorer citizens; and which, in order to understand the social revolution of the war, needs itself to be understood.

So let's imagine again. Let's swoop down on that other Britain, in which the black-and-white photographs of the time are such a true representative, for the sulphurous smoke that poured from the factories and the millions of chimneys was so dense that it not only obscured the sun and fouled the air, but lay its sticky residue on all that it touched. Every person, building, tree and blade of grass bore a sheath of its soot; and sometimes layer upon layer, year after year, so that if a building was cleaned, and the statues, swags of stone flowers and details of decoration uncovered, they were stared at with stunned disbelief.

So there we all were under black clouds in our black cities, with our black cars and black perambulators in which babies slept with soot-speckled faces. Is it any wonder, then, that with the damp and tainted air, many of us spluttered our way through the winter months, to greet the first haze of the spring sunshine with a feeling that we had survived against all the odds?

Here's a house in the East End of London: two rooms up and two rooms down in such disrepair that the roof leaks, damp rises like mercury, dry rot crumbles its skeleton, and the only water is from a tap in the yard. In winter, the kitchen houses its nine inhabitants until bedtime, for the only warmth is from a cooking stove heated by coal. Here they wash, bathe in a tin bath, cook, eat and relax under clotheslines of drying laundry. There are no washing machines or laundrettes, no central heating or constant hot water, no disposable nappies or drip-dry fabrics. A kettle is filled in the yard and boiled on the stove, where it jostles the stockpot and two or three heavy irons for pressing; and there is so much steam that the walls glisten with condensation which forms into runnels engorged with dirt. Because of the sulphurous fogs there's an annual spring-clean when every curtain, loose cover, counterpane and blanket is soaked and then washed in the tin bath or copper; and pray God it won't rain, because even in fine weather the wash can take two or three days to dry, by which time the smuts from the chimneys . . .

No wonder that London was nicknamed "the Smoke", and that it was smelt even before it was seen. After a holiday, and as the train approached the outskirts of London, I'd lean out of the window so as to savour the first whiff of that pungent and heady aroma; and when we puffed into Victoria Station with belches of smoke rising in fronds towards the encrusted roof, I'd shout for the sheer joy of being back home. But then I was born in the Smoke, and I was lucky.

Though a child of my time, and with the full complement of bronchitis, pneumonia, pleurisy, and the beginnings of tuberculosis, at least my mother could afford to pay for a doctor, medicine and an extra fire in the bedroom, let alone months in the pure air of a Swiss mountain. For others, it was cough-cough and grin-and-bear-it, accompanied by the ironic "It wasn't the cough that carried him off, but the coffin they carried him off in". But then, it was easy for a child of the slums to die, for there was little immunization or antibiotics. Diphtheria killed three to four thousand a year; whooping cough, two thousand; and tuberculosis, thirty to forty thousand, though not *all* of these were young.

I remember a cortège: leading it, a man pushed a pram handle attached to planks of wood suspended between two bicycle wheels, and which bore a small handmade coffin. Behind him walked a woman and a young girl, eyes staring and unfocused so as to distance themselves from the shame of such an outward show of their poverty. Goodbye dead child, whose first feeds had been flour and water because there was no money for milk and his mother's had dried up. And it wasn't the cough that carried him off, but making do with a bottle of mixture.

Hard to believe that, in my own childhood, a schoolfriend had had her tonsils removed on the kitchen table, and not because her parents were broke, but because that was how it was; just as the dentist haunted us because his drill dug out decay without an injection. One way and another, I remember a lot of pain. The knee that turned septic and had to be dressed for weeks; the gumboils and toothache; the children's surgical ward where dressings were changed behind a curtain, and we covered our ears to deaden the screams. Then, deformities were an everyday sight: crossed eyes and hare lips, and though there were artificial limbs, many couldn't cope and did the best they could with empty sleeves and crutches; just as most women couldn't afford the legal abortions that required two specialists to testify that the pregnancy was dangerous to their health, before being sent to an expensive nursing home. For the rest, it was a backstreet abortionist. Not that most of them were the ogres that they are now made out to be, and many women had nothing but praise for their services, for contraceptives were hard to come by and often regarded as shameful.

This, then, was the country where Paul Popper and his friends sought sanctuary, arriving in a London that was overcast and filthy, yet which possessed a zest that was as exhilarating as it was contagious. They stared at the sparkling, electrically-lit thoroughfares and shops, the buskers singing to the crowds and the queues at the theatres; the lamplighters bicycling through the side streets, swinging up poles to switch on the gaslamps; and the carts drawn by horses that clattered across the cobbles with harnesses jingling. Then there were the sounds. Before television ironed out our accents, Cockney was as thick as a peasouper; traders shouted their wares from stalls not yet confined to a few streets; and the barrel organs and beggars belted out songs: "Lily of Laguna", "Sally In Our Alley", "If You Were The Only Girl In The World", and most poignant of all, "Keep the Home Fires Burning". And last but by no means least, there were the smells: the horse dung steaming in the night air; the roasting chestnuts popping on the braziers; the belch of fish and chips as customers pushed out into the street; and, above all, the sweat of passengers in buses, trams and trains, for there were few anti-perspirants, and woollen clothes were expensive to clean. Not that many noticed, and if like me you were a child, then you could still smell the leather upholstery of a car as you knelt on the seat and stared out of the back window; and when you were taken to Piccadilly Circus, you stood nose-high to baskets of violets that were sold by old women called flower girls, and who perched in the shadow of Eros at the centre of the greatest Empire the world had ever known, and on which the sun would so very soon be setting.

CHAPTER
ONE

In the Beginning

War throws a long and haunting shadow, and for those of us who were children in the thirties, the Great War had the power to stun: the sightless men standing in doorways selling matches; the hard-won medals silting up the pawn shops; the old soldiers singing as they trudged the gutters because begging was a crime. But the heart of this shadow, the unique horror that was spoken of in the sepulchral tone usually reserved for the dead, was the legion of housebound men with not even the breath to speak above a whisper, let alone scream. The potency of their hidden suffering was the atom bomb of our time that, like children now, held the fascination of the worst that could ever happen.

Luckily for my ghoulish curiosity, Uncle Jack was so obsessed by his years in the trenches that he picked at his memories until the day of his death. It was the fading light that triggered the outbursts: I crouched on the rug that held coal specks that stuck to my knees, while he rocked in his armchair attacking the fire. Even then, he could only sidle up to the subject, poker rampant as he demonstrated the lunge of a bayonet or the ramming home of a shell. "Winter was hell," he'd announce. "Not that we were excused shaving, *and* in cold water, *and* with the wind whipping us sharper than any razor. I tell you, whatever else was muck, we'd cheeks like a baby's bottom when it came to Over the Top." Here he'd swing the poker towards the window, as if the Boche was even now crouched beyond the laburnum ready to pounce. "It was Over the Top and charge into No Man's Land, meaning smoke and screams; meaning corpses splayed on the wire; and God help us . . .". Here he'd break off, movement frozen and eyes turned glassy as if they'd been polished.

"Meaning *Mustard Gas*."

The terrible words lay between us like the canisters that had contained them, and he'd shudder and focus, shouting that I'd no right to egg him on when there were some things a child should never know. But we did know, desperately filling in the gaps from the talk of grown-ups. "Lungs as raw as a slice of liver", "Blisters so thick he could hardly swallow", "And from that day on he was a broken man".

And so it was that when a new war threatened, the government commissioned a secret report on the probable reaction to a gas attack, the findings of which predicted mass panic, an exodus to the countryside and widespread looting. Immediately accepting the worst of a people who gave it mandate, the government chose to reassure the public by ordering a gas mask for every man, woman and child in the British Isles. However, what it failed to predict was that such foresight in a usually slothful government would shock fear into the open, and sow the seeds of what was to become the miracle of wartime life: strangers, *British* strangers, actually talking to each other. Up and down the country, stiff upper lips grew mobile and words ran rampant. "We'll be in the front line, or why else have the buggers bothered", "There's no smoke without fire", and the ever-recurring and chilling prediction: "You do know we'll all be gassed!" Oh yes, we knew all right, even us children. Hadn't we been taken to the pictures to see Laurel and Hardy and Shirley Temple, and hadn't we caught the Gaumont British News reporting the Spanish Civil War? Worst of all, we'd heard the commentator booming over the scream of German and Italian bombers that they were target-practising for other and future wars. And if they'd stopped short of gas attacks, we had no trouble in anticipating what would happen to us. We'd be scrambling about in the gutters coughing our guts up; and those that weren't killed would be crippled for the rest of their pain-wracked lives. One thing was certain, the worst that could be imagined might very soon be fact.

When the gas masks were distributed, mine was issued at school. Pupils marched into the main hall, where we formed lines in front of the stage on which lolled an amorphous huddle of rubber contraptions from which bakelite windows peered, together with prehensile extensions through which we were told we'd be able to breathe. It was only the headmistress's flashing spectacles that kept me from bolting when my chin was thrust into a sinister bag, which was heaved over my head by iron fingers that tightened the straps until I was hermetically sealed within. Gasping for air, I was plunged into the smoke of No Man's Land as the window steamed up, and the stench of rubber was surely the gas that was even now eating into my liver lungs. I screamed. At least I tried to scream, but all that escaped was a *very* rude noise. I was farting through my head!

The sound was so unexpected and hilarious that the entire school fell about laughing, and any later efforts to save the population from mass slaughter was viewed by us children as a possible source of delight. We were right. The sudden outcrop of public air raid shelters might have been designed as headquarters for Cops and Robbers; the rattles that rent the air when grown-ups practised an Alert were toys that they'd played with at football matches; and as for the water tanks that sprang up in the streets, it was obvious that they'd been purpose-built for the sailing of paper boats.

On 3 September 1939, fifteen minutes after Britain declared war on Germany, the new and sinister air-raid sirens wailed across the country and everyone jumped for their lives. Adults tore round in demented circles, scrambling for gas masks that had long since been abandoned; while children were pushed into cupboards under the stairs, only to be hauled out again in favour of refuge under the dining-room table that hours earlier had served as a Wild West fort. That, for me, was when game and reality merged into one, and when the All Clear sounded with not a bomb in sight, it was obvious that the whole thing was a grown-ups' Let's Pretend. It continued to be Let's Pretend through the glorious autumn, when familiar figures started to strut about in uniforms that might have come out of some dressing-up box; while respectable mothers and their daughters appeared in trousers that up to then had been worn only at the seaside or by fast bits of fluff. Now they were commonplace, and not only because they were part of some uniform, but as protection against the cold during the non-existent air raids. It was but an extension of this to the siren suit: a dark, all-in-one garment along the line of rompers, often with elasticated cuffs, and with a zip which ran from the neck to below the waist. The theory behind the design was that it could be leapt into in seconds, and the wearer kept warm while rushing to the shelter and sitting for hours in its damp depths. What the male designers had failed to take into account was that unlike them we couldn't pull out our parts, so that the contrast between its snug interior and pulling the lot down before we could pee probably gave us more colds than if it hadn't been invented. Never mind, with stockings already in short supply, at least our legs were warm, and there was no ghastly gap between stocking top and knicker. Besides, siren suits were not only smart but allowed us to swagger, so that no female felt herself to be on a wartime footing until she was the proud possessor of the latest range.

As to the rest of the nation's clothing, like the white lines that the government slapped on curbs, lampposts, trees and mudguards of buses to help in the blackout, we festooned our persons not so much with touches of white, as barrages of the stuff; for though the enemy showed no sign of raining down death from above, it was more than likely that we'd be mown down in the ground-level blackness. Indeed, what had once been familiar streets now became surreal nightmares as the masked headlamps of cars and buses picked out dismembered parts of the public, who either belted for safety or positively courted disaster by hanging about and gawping upwards. The reason for this suicidal behaviour was that without street lighting, the moon and stars once more assumed their natural brilliance; while know-alls compounded the danger by grabbing passers-by to point out constellations that up to then had been dull diagrams on school blackboards. Then came the snow and the frost, transforming our already alien landscape into a fairy-tale country, where streets became silver snakes twisting between black canyons topped by roofs of glittering sugar, as against the skyline, churches and town halls were turned into battlements and towers for princesses.

If all things have a balance, then the splendour of those nights did much to compensate for the growing tattiness of the day. Parks were slashed with trenches and air-raid shelters; doors and windows cowed behind waterlogged sandbags that grew green with mildew and stank of cats; while the walls between were plastered with government notices: "No. 4 Shelter", "Fire Station", "Wardens' Post", and in more and more shop windows, the ubiquitous "Sold Out". They sold out of torches, batteries, thermos flasks, rugs, blackout material, black dye, hardboard, and sticky paper to hold blasted window-panes; until finally, anything that was warm or remotely useful was rationed or disappeared.

As the streets developed their wartime face, so did our gardens, where a fine crop of shelters replaced chrysanthemums and dahlias. Named after the Home Secretary, the Anderson shelter arrived as sheets of corrugated iron that had to be bolted together, the resulting tunnel with doors at each end for easy escape, planted in the earth to a depth of four feet, and topped off with fifteen inches of soil that the fanatical gardener covered with flowers, or, if really inspired, a gnome or two and a wishing well. Humped like an ancient burial ground, it was designed to hold six people, though in acute discomfort and often filling with water, but it was a splendid rendezvous for marauding gangs of animals and children. Far more popular was the indoor Morrison shelter, an oblong steel box with mesh sides that could serve as a table during the day, and the modern equivalent of a four-poster at night. Luckiest of all were the owners of a cellar where, after strengthening the ceiling with props, a family could spend a reasonable night warmed by a paraffin stove and even lit by electricity.

However, whatever the type of shelter, it had to be inspected by the street air-raid warden, so that in the event of a direct hit, Heavy Rescue would know where to dig people out. It was during this time when nothing much seemed to be happening that air-raid wardens replaced tax inspectors as public enemy number one, for not only did they demand entry into what had once been the Englishman's castle, but they could insist on alterations if the place of safety fell below government guidelines. For this nosy-parkering they were paid the princely sum of £3 a week, the rest of their time being spent hanging about and brewing up. No wonder that the public fumed with indignation, when they were either busy making their home impregnable, or belting about in every direction.

What had begun months earlier as a trickle of expatriates returning from overseas, in the first week of war became a flood. Hurrying for the safety of a country they still called Home, they locked their houses, handed the keys to the British Embassy, before struggling on to trains with all the luggage they could carry; while passing them on the way out, enemy aliens had five days' grace to return to *their* homeland. Add to this the thousands of men who had been called up and were travelling to camps; the million and a half children officially evacuated; the many more who made their own arrangements, and often with a following caravan of pets and furniture; as well as the thousands of organizations, businesses, private schools, government departments, contents of museums and art galleries that were flung to all parts of the British Isles, and it's a miracle that our roads and railways didn't combust from the friction of hurtling vehicles. As it was, ancient charabancs were dusted down and added to fleets of buses, trains were packed to suffocation, were late departing and even later arriving, or were shunted into sidings because of troop movements; while the few who owned cars were begged to make return journeys in order to shift their relations, neighbours and friends.

Whatever the means of this manic musical chairs, most of the travellers shared one thing in common: they were leaving the familiar for the unknown, and the adrenalin engendered by both fear and anticipation stimulated even the most withdrawn into talking non-stop to anyone else who paused to draw breath. In the same vein, the government communicated non-stop through a deluge of paper and through the radio. There were exhortations, regulations, information, and the registration and issuing of identity and ration cards. You name it, we listened to it, read it, filled it in or wrote to ask what was meant by the small print. Add to this the change of address incurred by a third of the population, it's no wonder that the increase in mail was 1000 per cent, particularly as firms and individuals evacuated to God-knows-where were desperately trying to make contact, if not sense, with God-knows-who. In such disorientation, it is hardly surprising that the nation turned to that last bastion of immobile certainty, the BBC News.

So there we all were, charging about and writing or talking our heads off, until, at the witching hour of nine o'clock in the evening, the voice of the BBC cast a spell over the nation and it froze to listen. To be out and about in the blacked-out and empty streets was an unearthly experience. From every inhabited building came the lone voice of a newsreader, his report echoing through hamlets and cities, over mountains and across valleys, and on and on to the furthest shore of our island. The precious words were our sanity, our news from Carthage, and our Song of Songs.

Advertising, though a far less august source of information, was equally reliable, for a business has no axe to grind aside from selling a product, and that demands an instant and accurate response to the smallest changes in attitude. But first, let's go back to the preoccupations of pre-war Britain, so as to have a bench mark. Combing through middle-of-the-road magazines, I was flabbergasted by the country's obsession with it's bodily functions, and in particular the dangerous substances coursing through it's alimentary canal. Here are two beauties:

> Unless two pints of bile juice flow from your liver into your bowels every day, your movements get hard and constipated and your food decays unnaturally in your twenty-eight feet of bowels. This decay sends poison all over your body in six minutes. It makes you gloomy . . . your friends smell this decay coming out of your mouth.

> Unless bowels move regularly, your child will be weakly, peevish, dull and stunted.

With such dire warnings, it's no wonder that mothers and nannies lived in constant terror of their charges not being "regular". First thing in the morning, the tiny tots were asked "Have you been?", which meant "to the lavatory". If not, they were told to "Go out and come in nicely", meaning "Try again". If the poor child was still unsuccessful, then it was "bound", which did *not* mean it was trussed up but that its bowels were in bondage, and had to be flushed through with one of a multitude of medicines, including Angier's Brand Emulsion, Syrup of Figs, Carter's Little Liver Pills and Andrew's Liver Salts. An interesting corollary to this is that our present-day leaders over sixty were brought up on the inflexible routine of being "regular" and, if not purged, which must surely account for their longing to return to the certainty of Victorian values and the efficacy of the short sharp shock. Aside from Inner Cleanliness, another pre-war obsession was personal hygiene — hardly surprising when there were few anti-perspirants, and no antibiotics to cure blood poisoning, which was a killer. Even so, the drama with which the advertisements rammed home their message, makes our present-day version but a pallid shadow.

> The knife slips . . . a trifling cut . . . a speck of dirt . . . blood poisoning . . . months in hospital . . . maybe even AMPUTATION! Why risk it? Use John Knight's Family Health toilet soap!

To underline the authenticity of these messages, they were often accompanied by a drawing or photograph of medical experts; the nurses in starched collars and flowing headgear who were serenely beautiful or reassuring and motherly, while the doctors suggested Harley Street specialists by their winged collars and striped trousers. Sometimes the doctor sported a small moustache reminiscent of Herr Hitler's, and though probably subliminal, it did play on the pre-war belief that the Hitler Youth were clean-limbed and superbly healthy. After all, with not a pimple in sight, it was odds-on that the Führer had got to grips with something as indisciplined as a sluggish bowel.

As indelicate as were the advertisements when it came

to the nation's bowels, they could only hint at the link between God, Hygiene and Sex that Dr Arnold had banged on about in his school. "Cleanliness is next to Godliness for the clean-living man" was all that they dared to allow themselves, when "clean living" was the euphemism for not putting yourself about with the opposite sex. However, for those who couldn't resist the weakness of the flesh and needed contraceptions and pills, the copywriters invented coded messages that would not have shamed the Secret Service. Rendells' products disguised their vaginal cap under the heading "feminine hygiene", and Damaroids advertised virility pills with the splendidly patriotic title of "The Great British Rejuvenator"!

Once at war, the old standbys continued to flourish, but were joined by many new advertisements, some of them appearing in the personal column of newspapers. Jewish refugees, who had fled from Nazi persecution and arrived here penniless, advertised their Services as domestic servants, though many possessed degrees; and there was a flood of advertisements for flats and houses in safe areas, including this typical up-market let in Norfolk: "Georgian residence in spotless condition. 3 recept., 7 beds, dressing-room, 2 baths, kitchen, garden, paddock 2½ acres. Excellent sport, yachting. £1,850 p.a." Nor were pets forgotten, and for those who hadn't been destroyed because of the fear of bombing, Captain Holdsworth, MC, recommended his Boxhill Kennels as absolutely safe for dogs and cats; and at Henley-on-Thames, the Segry Kennels had room for "a few more evacuated dogs".

During the early months of the war, most advertising copy remained unchanged, though sometimes prefaced by a reference to altered conditions. For instance, the public was warned to safeguard its childrens' health while away from home, and one manufacturer made the bizarre and mysterious statement: "Strange children — Scrubbs Ammonia for evacuees"; while even that doyen of authority, the medical expert, was joined by the Forces. A handsome male officer recommended Wright's Coal Tar Soap, while Gibbs Dentifrice announced that their toothpaste was the stuff to give the troops; but then, having no particular trade, the Forces could be used to promote anything. A WAAF had a "pen for her thoughts" made by Stephens; the AFS preferred Gold Flake cigarettes; and Brylcreem's dressing for hair was no longer displayed on famous cricketers, but on the RAF, who sported their forage caps at a 90° angle to the head, and needed a stiffened wave to underpin the gravity-defying headgear. This campaign was so successful that the public renamed the RAF the "Brylcreem Boys" — a title that was not entirely complimentary, and from the lips of the Army or Navy, downright insulting.

Amongst the many changing conditions, the blackout was a godsend. TCP cured the stress and strain that made colds harder to shake off; Dr Cassels announced that his tablets were a cure for blackout nerves; and Famel Brand Syrup conquered coughs caused by blacked-out nights and closed windows. As for the animals, Bob Martin's Hysteria Pills for dogs were "an important item of ARP", while Postroy's flea and lice powder played on the growing chauvinism by advising the readers to "rid your dog of foreigners"!

And so it went on, every change in wartime conditions being mirrored in the advertisements, though I'm delighted to say that our manufacturers remained loyal to the belief that the health of the nation was, in the last analysis, dependent on the regularity of the British bowel!

The liver should pour out 2 pints of liquid bile into your bowels daily. If the bile is not flowing freely, your food doesn't digest. It just decays in your bowels. Gas bloats up your stomach, your whole system is poisoned and you feel sour, sunk, and the world looks *punk*.

So long live Carter's Little Liver Pills, whose clairvoyant vision extended even unto the youth of today.

CHAPTER
TWO

The Weather

The rest of the world has a climate, we have the Weather: an unpredictable force that lets loose snow in June, hail in August, and a heatwave come November. When the weather can change by the minute and within a few miles, it's little wonder that the British are obsessed with it, greet their friends with news of it, and feel a smug satisfaction when the forecaster announces that it is the heaviest rainfall/snowfall/longest drought since records began.

I have a theory that we owe our record number of eccentrics and poets to it, for until the Greenhouse Effect, we had no outdoor cafés to lure a potential bard or nutter into exchanging strongly held views until they melted into a consensus bereft of individuality, let alone passion. No. Up to a few years ago, our young people were so poorly paid that they couldn't afford the conviviality of a pub, and were driven to hurrying down inhospitable streets and into the forcing house of their solitary rooms. Given the boredom of such a routine, what more natural than that they escaped into a fantasy world of poetry and prose. And if they lacked a talent for literature, then they stared at the walls and brooded, their thoughts solidifying into obsessions, or taking wild flights that given a few short years could blossom into the glory of a mild and engaging madness.

However, in times of war, no such indulgence is possible, for the young are there to do battle and are winkled out of homes or digs into the rip-roaring life of the shelters, barrack rooms, civic restaurants, queues for food, and all kinds of other and unnatural practices; and I am convinced that it was this forced and yet happy comradeship that has underlined memories of the forties, and made them so much sharper than anything since.

On the outbreak of war I exchanged the tranquillity of a London flat for the cut and thrust of a village, that killed for ever my town-dweller's belief in rustic harmony. Church distrusted Manor, locals suspected evacuees, and the council was on non-speaking terms with any other council whose boundaries marched with its own. And then came the winter of '39/40, a winter so terrible that the village, like the nation, was driven to unite if only to survive. First came the snow, and then the frost, and then the rain and yet more frost, until the sombre landscape was transformed into a carpet of diamonds that was as breathtaking as it was lethal. Under the winter sun, every twig, every hedgerow, every blade of grass glittered with a frosting of ice that turned the fields into beds of nails, the roads into glass, and froze the feet of the birds to their perches. Even to venture out was to tempt death, and the old fell in their thousands, their broken bones filling the beds in every hospital and Outpatients — if, that is, a telephone call could reach an ambulance, and the ambulance reach its victim. Between my godmother's house and Marlborough, the weight of ice brought down so many telegraph wires that the road seemed to be fringed with the rigging of shipwrecks; while in the fields beyond, the animals petrified into statues. And oh, the enveloping silence! Not a vehicle swished past and not a branch whispered, though an occasional crash marked the fall of a tree under its glassy weight.

In the bewildering cold, black silhouettes picked their way through a white wilderness, desperately searching for kindling that might be hacked from the ground; while the vegetables needed a blowtorch to soften the brick-hard earth before a pickaxe could prize them free. Cut off from the outside world, save for planes dropping us food and feed for the animals, our only contact was through the radio, its voice of doom speaking of vast areas cut off, the Thames frozen over, thousands of animals missing or dead, miners unable to hew coal, and machinery grinding to a hault. Any uplifting news was saved until last, the listeners regaled with tales of heroism and fortitude so as to remind us that, compared with some, our life was a bed of roses. Translated this meant "Don't grumble", an instruction that was as ridiculous as it was futile. "I grumble, therefore I am" could be the nation's motto, for over the centuries we have honed our complaints into an art that is as pleasurable as it is comforting.

The classic grumble comes in two parts, first the boast and then the irritation: "I've survived the worst winter in living memory, but that's no excuse for the Gas/Electricity/Water Board to tell me that I must wait, when others I won't mention have been reconnected!" To this typical example, the war added an answer that was as maddening as it was irrefutable: "Don't you know there's a war on", carrying a sadistic smugness that drove many to blows, and I well remember my mother announcing that if I ever said it again, she'd requisition my sweet ration and scoff the lot.

Even so, it was "Don't you know there's a war on" that forced our village into becoming an unlikely model of co-operation. Church and Manor banded together to distribute food, the council loaned its only snow-plough to its erstwhile enemy, and the local children and evacuees swept the paths of the old and infirm. In fact, by the time the thaw had set in, the weather had achieved what the government was still trying to encourage: communal co-operation and the pooling of resources. But then, war and our weather have much in common for they are equally unpredictable, so perhaps it was the weather that prepared the nation to accept the vagaries of years of privation, and with a phlegmatism that surprised even us.

As the war continued, and food and our fatty covering grew lean, the cold and the damp took their dispiriting toll; in fact whenever I picture those times, it is always against a backdrop of winter. There must have been springs and summers, but all I can recall is the odd sunny day, and then only because something memorable happened. Indeed I well remember deliberately turning a blind eye to the beauties of nature, which by contrast only heightened the chaos of our lives and made them unbearable. No, better the grey day attuned to all the other privations, and which could turn the discomfort of the wardens' or army post into a cosy haven of welcome. Besides, most people worked so hard and for such long hours, that it was infuriating to see the sun and not be able to bask in it.

If peace is a sunny upland, then war is a damp shelter, a queue for food in an east wind, and trudging icy miles when the transport had broken down. Even that universal comforter, the hot bath, no longer wrought its magic, for more than five inches of water was unpatriotic, so that while bottoms glowed in the unnatural warmth, shoulders and faces froze, and teeth chattered from the draught of a window or door loosened by bomb blast. Then, too, we were often exhausted and that makes you feel the cold, for it was not unusual to spend a fitful night in the shelter, work twelve hours, then spend more hours travelling home to do the chores, before preparing for yet another night of interrupted dozing.

It was during the Blitz, followed by the intermittent bombing, that the nation learnt to read its future in the elements, for enemy air attacks depended on reasonable conditions. Once again the full moon took on its ancient and sinister aura, when by its light, enemy bombers could spot their target, while thick cloud, that had once been so depressing, promised a reasonable night's sleep; though if it rained and then cleared, the pilots could pick out the shining streets and know they were over a built-up area.

Sadly, what was good for the town-dwellers often conflicted with the farmers. Cut off from supplies from Europe and the East, and with our tonnage sinking in the Atlantic, the country became more and more dependent on growing its own food, and what had once been called a bad harvest now became a disaster. Daily, the newspapers reported the gathering of crops, and if it rained during this time, then everyone waited with bated breath, for it could mean a cut in the bread ration, lack of winter feed for the animals and the dearth of vegetables with which we filled ourselves. For this reason, many reverted to the ways of their ancestors, watching for the portents of a fine summer: how high the birds were nesting, when the May tree blossomed, the movement of frogs which signalled a drought, and all the other half-remembered old wives' tales that had once been greeted with such derision. "Rain before seven, fine before eleven", "Red sky at night, shepherd's delight; Red sky in the morning, shepherd's warning", and if it rained on the day of St Swithin's, God help the lot of us!

As the war years passed, the nation became attuned to the slightest shift in the weather, for with little central heating, and none in the buses, trains and few cars, we all shared the same conditions, just as we shared the same dream of peace: the sunny uplands of an idyllic life free from the damp and the cold.

It was not to be. In the peacetime winter of 1947 it was the coldest February and the wettest March since records began, and to worse effect than in '39. Worn out by war and the disappointments of peace, we stared out at the elements and despaired.

Again, animals died in their thousands, coal remained in the ice-fisted earth, and such vast areas were cut off that one village was near starvation. As for transport: the Channel was impassable, the main North-South road was blocked, and drifts twenty-foot high trapped buses and trains. With the lack of coal supplies, gas and electricity had to be so drastically reduced that government offices, banks and the Law Courts were forced to struggle on by candlelight. After years of fighting, the effects of the weather were far worse than the winter of '39, for there were thousands of homeless; broken-down rolling stock could not be replaced; there was little lead or iron to mend burst pipes; factories that had once made fires had not yet returned to peacetime production; and without the target of a war to be won, high purpose was replaced by stoic endurance, so that we drifted through the icy wastes as aimlessly as the old who have forgotten where they are going.

I was living in a basement flat in London, where I'd wake in a bedroom that was so cold that my breath steamed, and when I switched on the fire it was almost too frail to be seen. Shivering, I'd have to wait twenty minutes for the kettle to boil for a cup of tea, before setting off on a nightmare journey to work. Once there, there was still no respite, everyone huddled over desks in mittens and coats or officer British warms with their paler patches where the rank had been removed.

This was when the naval duffle coat became so popular. Offloaded by the government into ex-service stores, they were a godsend with their hoods and thick material, and many tramped the streets looking like hooded figures out of a medieval painting. Even the West End of London, that had once been such a jolly and glamorous place, now looked like a transit camp: gutters banked with impacted snow to a height of three feet; shop windows still boarded up from bomb blast because glass was so scarce; soot-encrusted buildings with flaking pre-war paint; and the gallant horses that had pulled vehicles throughout the war, buckling on icy streets across which passers-by carried the old.

After work and the misery of the return journey, I'd stagger into the freezing flat and stand on the damp flagstones of the lean-to kitchen trying to cook. Because everyone else was doing the same, the pressure of gas was so low that the flame "plopped" continuously, and had to be lighted over and over again. At last, and still in my coat, I'd huddle over a tepid fire, eating a tepid meal of reconstituted egg or a sliver of meat or whale steak or the revolting Barracuda, before braving the arctic waste of my bedroom and the enfolding ice of the sheets.

Though many were convinced that we'd entered a new

ice age and would never again see the spring, at last the black clouds parted and revealed an anaemic sun that slowly melted the snow and icicles that hung like chimes from every burst pipe. Now it seemed as if the whole world was dissolving, as drips joined runnels that trickled into streams that coursed into rivers of waste that blocked and then overran the gutters; while above us, wedges of snow thundered on to the pavements and passersby. And when at last the city emerged, it was as if a bridal veil had been lifted to reveal the face of a battered and ancient crone; but beauty is in the eye of the beholder, so that all we saw were her dear and familiar features.

I emerged from my basement flat like a shade from the underworld. Around me, neighbours huddled together in groups, blinking in the unfamiliar light. "It's all over," we whispered, as we crossed our fingers in case we were tempting fate, for we all knew that when it came to the British weather, nothing is ever certain.

CHAPTER
THREE

Transport

I've always had a passion for trains, and I'm sure that this is because my first sighting was in the 1930s when they reached their peak of perfection.

Not for me the "rationalization" of present-day transport, when trains speed past abandoned stations, picking us up from one city and dumping us in another, stomachs engorged with powdered coffee, or enduring the greater obscenity of boiling water poured into a plastic cup in which tea-bag and powdered milk have already been mixed, and what's more, which has to be carried through crowded carriages where the muck slops over, burning fingers and staining clothes. Now, at journey's end, I'm not only queasy and damp, but exhausted by the so-called air conditioning, after lolling in a carriage that is far too hot and with not a chance of opening a window. As for the area managers to whom the public is invited to complain! Aside from not having sighted one yet, who could trust those enormous faces staring down from the British Rail posters, when most of them look half-baked or downright criminal and not a uniform to be seen. No, as far as I'm concerned, travel today is something I've been forced to go through, like the customs and adolescence.

But oh the thirties: then the station master not only dared to show his face, but was a proud figure in a knife-sharp starched collar, a uniform covered with gold braid and wearing an important hat. Under his benign and godlike gaze, who could not feel cherished? But best of all was the train itself: the might of a steam engine with its polished brass and its shrieks of steam, and which pulled cosy carriages that seated eight passengers, above whose heads watercolours illustrated all the many exciting places the public might visit. For the rich in the first-class carriages there were starched linen headrests with embroidered initials of the line; and all had electric light instead of fluorescent strips that sometimes make passengers look as if they're recovering from a mysterious and debilitating complaint. Then, even the doors had a special sound, and when the porters slammed them, the brass fitments engaged with a mellow echo that was as reassuring as the start of the journey was thrilling: fierce whistles, followed by belches of smoke and a clack-clack of the wheels going ever faster as the train puffed out of the station with all the assurance of a conqueror. By the time passengers had inspected the rows of terraced houses, the back gardens, and with any luck an occasional room whose light was on, a white-coated steward was walking the corridors ringing a brass bell and shouting "First sitting for tea"; and when a customer entered the restaurant car, it was to be greeted by walls of inlaid wood, the intimate lighting of individual art deco lamps at every table, and the glory of the tea itself: unconstrained tea leaves in a pot, real milk, hot water, a sugar basin with *tongs*, toast and jam and Dundee cake, and all of it served by waiters in gold-braided jackets or starched coats.

So, the customers ate their tea, while the train stopped at stations and halts that vied with each other for the best display of flowers, some of them planted so that they spelt out the place name, and with white stones marking the borders; and because the windows opened, passengers were regaled with the smells of the country, or the first heady whiff of the sea. All right, so there were smuts and smoke, especially in tunnels, but surely that was a small price to pay when in every other respect even the lowliest of travellers was made to feel important, for it was the sole job of an LMS employee to look after the theatrical touring companies.

As for the tube trains, they were as smart as fresh paint. Lights behind frosted glass shells flattered the passengers, who sat on red and green upholstered seats with real leather arms, while the carriages and stations were hung with posters that were designed by the top artists of the day. Indeed, London Transport won so many awards for these posters that now they are shown in art exhibitions all over the world.

This then was railway travel until 1939, and though it was the war that began the decline, personally I will never forgive Dr Beeching for giving it the *coup de grâce* that cut off so many small towns and villages, and led to the final insult of paring that most romantic of words "Railway" to the banality of "Rail".

During the last weeks of peace and the first months of war, every form of transport was pressed into service for the massive exodus of people, businesses, institutions and goods to a safe area, by far the largest group being the government's evacuation of children to reception centres throughout the country. As early as the spring of 1940, buses and especially trains were showing signs of wear. However, the country had more important things to do than minor repairs, and as long as the trains got from A to B, that was all that mattered. Besides, many of the repair shops and coach builders had switched to war work, while there was such a cutback in cleaners and railway staff because of the Call Up, that the niceties that had made travelling such a pleasure were already beginning to disappear. As for the stations, fires in the waiting-rooms were intermittent or non-existent, and the gaily coloured posters were covered with bleak notices instructing passengers to do this, and not to do that, and "Is Your Journey Really Necessary?" had begun to madden us all. As if anyone would travel if they didn't have to, when the trains were increasingly filthy, packed to overflowing, and often stopping and starting for no apparent reason. Sometimes they stopped in the empty countryside far from any signal, when indignant faces would pop out of windows and shout to harassed guards, as the more adventurous jumped out and wandered about, sure that the start would be so slow that they'd be able to jump on again. This was not always the case, the demon driver suddenly taking off and leaving the odd passenger to fend for himself.

Travelling by night was the worst. Nothing could be seen by the light of bulbs painted dark blue because of the blackout, so that no one could read or write letters. People just sat squashed together, heads lolling on strangers' shoulders, and with feet propped on luggage and kit bags because Servicemen were stretched out on the luggage racks; and when you had to go to the lavatory, it was an assault course. First the carriage door had to be prised open — no easy matter when someone was jammed against it on the other side — then the corridor had to be negotiated: lines of exhausted passengers leaning against the rails across the windows, many with their bottoms propped against the facing wall, and who were not best pleased to be asked to move, while scattered across the floor was yet more luggage on which the lower tier of passengers huddled and slept; and when finally the lavatory *was* sighted, there was always a line of indignant passengers, the first in the queue thundering on the door because the occupant had fallen asleep or was hiding from the ticket collector. When at long, long last the train stopped at what you thought was your station, it was almost impossible to verify, for all place names had been removed in case of invasion, and people were reluctant to confirm or deny anything when they might be giving away information of national importance.

From the moment the Blitz began, railways were one of the main objectives, and travelling became chaotic, until at one point many of the London termini were out of action simultaneously and people slept in the forecourts hoping against hope that somehow they'd get away.

Here is the story of one journey. For the Christmas holidays, my friend and I had to travel from our school in Devon to her home on the Kintyre peninsula in the West of Scotland. The train to London was so slow that we missed our connection to Glasgow, and had to spend the night in an air raid shelter in the Marble Arch tube. The next day, after breakfast with a naval officer much impressed by our sang-froid, we telephoned our parents telling them not to worry, before catching a bus to Euston. The station was that odd wartime mish-mash of the old grandeur of an enormous and colonnaded booking hall, plus makeshift passages of salvaged wood plastered with notices, including a blackboard announcing cancelled trains due to bombing on the line, and the ominous graffiti: "Hitler's cooking in the buffet"! Like all forecourts, Euston's was seething with the Services of all nations, civilians, the WVS serving buns, and the station staff pushing trolleys of the Royal Mail or steaming tea urns, and through which we had to drag our luggage and ourselves, for there were no trolleys and porters had disappeared.

Ours was a night journey: over *seventeen* hours of stopping and starting through a frozen landscape and, what's more, under a full moon, when a moving train was a gift to enemy bombers. The carriage was packed, filthy, dark and unheated, and we arrived in Glasgow having not eaten or drunk, distinctly grubby and in the middle of a snowstorm. From there we took a train to the coast for a boat to the isles, but when we arrived it was to join a crowd sitting on the banks of the Clyde, for the last boat before Christmas had been cancelled. By an amazing stroke of good luck, one of the Kintyre fishing boats was in port, and what's more captained by our good friend Denny Mackintosh. To the generous cheers of the stranded, the two of us climbed aboard, together with a nubile beauty not averse to Denny's many charms. I was deeply honoured when he asked me to take the wheel while he went below. Goodness, I felt heroic: the lone schoolgirl, captain of all she surveyed, sailing down the Clyde in the moonlight. Some time later, the real captain emerged and went berserk. I had been told to hold the course by lining up a point on the bow with a distant peak, but I've never been much good at directions, and had lined up with the wrong peak and sailed slap-bang through a minefield. Still, "A miss is as good as a mile," as I told him, and some time later we arrived at our destination after a journey of over two days! When I told my mother, she kept muttering that I might have killed myself, and when I replied, "Don't you know there's a war on?" she was distinctly ratty.

After Dunkirk and the later entry of the United States into the war, foreign service personnel added to the congestion of the trains, so that to find a seat was a major triumph. On a forty-eight-hour pass from my army camp, I'd think nothing of spending up to twelve hours standing in a corridor that was either freezing or so hot that the smell of sweat rising from service shirts was as pungent as it was unnecessary, for it was a chargeable offence to remove ties or open top buttons.

Buses were far less of an ordeal, if only that the journeys were shorter. However, they too had their risks, for with so many streets bombed, the buses had flexible routes, and would take off through side streets, zig-zagging around craters in the finest tradition of motorbike scrambles. On top of this, there was the blackout, and a journey that had once taken ten minutes could last anything up to an hour. Still, there was always the glorious talk, which was led by the conductor in the same manner as the host of a chat show today. "Ladies and gentlemen, due to an unexploded bomb, we are today taking the scenic route through Belgrave Square, so if any of you want Hyde Park you'd better nip off smartish." The speech would then open up into a description of the raid the night before, followed by the personal reminiscences of the passengers, and often taking off into the wild blue yonder. It was always good-humoured, and a wonderful glimpse into other people's lives, for with few cars, all stratas of society were represented, and with so much shared there was a camaraderie that can never have been equalled before or since. After all, how many now have ever glimpsed a politician on public transport, let alone a famous actor or city magnate?

Initially, cars had a basic petrol ration, but in 1940 this was abolished, except for special cases such as doctors and the heads of emergency services. In order to stop black marketeering or misuse, petrol for farm machinery was dyed, and police would dip-stick tanks to check that there had been no siphoning-off. My great-uncle, a farmer, whose lone machine had broken down, had the bright idea of boring holes in the back of his ancient Austin 7, through which my prone great-aunt pushed seed as he drove up and down the fields. However, because this was a car, and though never used on the road, my uncle feared that he'd be prosecuted for using dyed petrol. Always law-abiding, he wrote to the Minister of Transport explaining the position and asking for dispensation. To its eternal credit, and despite far more important matters like winning the war, his letter was discussed in the Commons, and he received an official blessing. His son has the Minister's letter to this day, for as my uncle remarked, when democracy makes the time to discuss the plight of just one citizen, then it deserves to win any battle against a dictatorship.

With driving for pleasure banned, the treasured family car was laid up in the garage, having first had its tyres removed to preserve them, before being propped up on bricks and further immobilized by the removal of the rotor arm. Indeed, because of the fear of invasion and enemy spies, drivers were instructed to immobilize any car when it was left, and many a driver was seen tearing his hair because he couldn't find the tiny but essential piece of his engine.

Without cars and with public transport so crowded, many

took to bicycles, though like much else they were in short supply, and it was not uncommon to see someone peddling by on a model that had been bought in the First World War. When they broke down, which was often, the owner could be heard to mutter that he'd give his eyeteeth for one of the streamlined folding bicycles that the Germans carried when they parachuted on to Holland. However, this sounded so far-fetched that most discounted it as rumour. Most were wrong.

With all the many problems of transport, people chose to walk whenever they could and often for long distances, for aside from the danger of falling into craters, walking in the city became a real pleasure. Once the railings around the squares had been removed for scrap, there was the joy of resting on grass that had been forbidden; and with so many buildings demolished, unfamiliar and often breathtaking views were revealed, so that, together with the decrease in traffic, walking became one of the few bonuses of the bombing.

If there is one memory that those of us who lived through the war will never forget, it was the reunions and farewells at the stations. Arriving on leave, Service personnel would dash helter-skelter down the platforms and into the open arms of loved ones, the crowds turning to smile at their joyous shouts. But for the separations, everything was reversed. Amidst crowds that averted their eyes, silent couples and families clutched each other as if they were drowning, men and women crying as they kissed, or simply staring. Eyes, noses and mouths were minutely examined: the line of a jaw, the way the hair fell over a forehead, the sweet curve of a cheek. This is his, this is her face, and if, God forbid, anything happens, I'll never forget.

But if they were killed, the bereaved were torn by guilt because somehow they had forgotten. "I can see the eyes and mouth," they'd confess, "but the whole face — it just seems to disintegrate." Only in dreams were the features reassembled, to slip away again as surely as the train that took them, once the mourner awoke.

By the end of the war, every form of transport had been repaired or botched together, until it seemed that it moved "on a wing and a prayer", as the RAF so poetically put it. But it did keep moving, and besides much else, it somehow managed to carry a swollen population, all the machinery essential for victory, and the food that we grew to feed the nation. Finally, the children were brought home, many of them six years older than when they had left their families, who waited, as so many before had waited, eyes straining for the first sight of their loved ones.

CHAPTER
FOUR

Bombing

After Germany invaded and subsequently defeated Poland, Hitler's onslaught ceased, and some in Britain began to mutter that the war would be all over by Christmas. They should have known better, for their parents had used the very same words in 1914.

As autumn darkened into winter, Russia — then Germany's ally — invaded Finland; and though Britain was appalled, all the government felt able to offer the Finns was sympathy. Indeed, such was our lack of commitment to all-out war that Neville Chamberlain's government chose not to bomb the German munition factories, on the grounds that they were private property. Though this shameful decision was kept secret, the public sensed the ambiguous attitude of the industrialists and much of the Establishment, whose vested interest had pressed the theory that if we didn't bomb enemy factories, they wouldn't bomb ours! Given such reasoning on top of little decisive action by us or the allies, it's no wonder that in the spring and early summer of 1940 Hitler was confident that his forces could conquer Western Europe. In a breathtaking *blitzkrieg*, Germany first attacked Norway and Denmark, then overran Holland, Belgium and Luxembourg, and, finally and unbelievably, France. Day after day, the German Army and Air Force devastated a country whose roads were so engorged with fleeing refugees, that the headlong retreat of the French and British armies as they sought to evade encirclement was obstructed, and lines of communication cut, so that the movement of many troops became instinctive rather than being directed by a masterplan.

It was during this period, as the people in Britain watched from the sidelines with a sense of increasing impotence, that two unrelated events brought about an extraordinary and revitalizing change in the heart of the nation. The first was the fighting talk of our new leader, Winston Churchill. Not for him the compromising and mealy-mouthed words of Chamberlain, but the glorious English of our forefathers that rolled off his tongue like a roar. How we loved him when, instead of placating our fears, he announced that all he had to offer was blood, toil, tears and sweat; that we would fight to the last man to defeat the evils of the Third Reich, and not just for our own skins, but for the whole of the civilized world!

Following on the heels of this boost to our morale, the second event unrolled, and again we watched incapable of action. The Germans had been so successful in their drive across France that they had pushed our Army back until it was trapped on the beaches of Dunkirk on the Northern Coast. Their capture seemed certain. Then, and by what seemed a miracle of good weather, our soldiers and many of our allies were literally pulled from the sea; and not just by the Navy, but by hundreds of small ships that had volunteered their services from ports as far afield as Devon and Yorkshire. It was as if the anger generated by our months of impotence had suddenly burst, and with such a force that it drove that bravest of fleets through the very jaws of enemy bombardment. Stunned by the audacity and heroism of the crews, we learnt that old men and boys had crammed soldiers onto their decks until they were only inches above the water, and that many had not only made it back to England, but refuelled and returned as many as *seven* times. In a few days, over 335,000 soldiers were saved, including over 100,000 Frenchmen, their feet hardly touching the ground before an army of civilians rushed to their aid. The women's voluntary Services wrapped them in blankets and handed out tea, soup and sandwiches; buses and trains were re-scheduled, and dispersed the rescued to Holding Units and hospitals into which nurses and doctors had poured; while across the country at railway stations and halts, locals gathered with refreshments in case a train might stop, many throwing food into carriage windows when they failed to do so. And when at last the final man had been helped ashore, there surged through the country an unreasonable and exhilarating relief. The time of watching and uncertainty was over. We knew that we stood alone, and that in the battle and possible invasion ahead, every man, woman and child would have some part to play.

These then were the two events — Churchill's leadership and Dunkirk — that tempered the nation to withstand the horrors that were to come so soon; for, as the summer promised to outstrip the glory of '39, the long-awaited enemy planes thundered across the country and the bombs rained down. First the Channel approaches and the ports of Southern England were targeted, and then the airfields, aircraft factories and other industrial sites; and when London was bombed and the RAF retaliated by bombing Berlin, everyone knew that this was only the beginning, for Hitler was nothing if not a man of revenge.

How to describe the fear and the camaraderie of those endless nights? I was at a boarding school in Bristol, which was far enough West to have been considered safe by our parents. However, Hitler must have regarded our school as fair game, if only because we were central to the docks, an airfield and factories. At the first wail of the siren, we filed out of the dormitory and into the hall, where Matron checked us off in the register and made sure we wore dressing gowns and slippers, before we *walked* down to the cellar, for running as well as talking was forbidden. Not that anything could be heard above the distant bombardment, but rules were rules, and Matron kept watch on our mouths for any breach of school discipline. Because the cellar was out of bounds, we thought it a wonderfully mysterious place, and would prop ourselves against the bins of pickled eggs, too excited to notice the crunch as approaching sticks of bombs exploded; and when they became too ear-splitting to be ignored, our gym mistress would raise her arms and lead us in rousing choruses of "One Man Went To Mow" and "Row, Row, Row Your Boat", which were belted out with such abandon that we all but drowned the enemy action. Possibly because our fear of appearing sissy was greater even than death, I can't remember anyone breaking down, only of being self-consciously jolly in the mould of "Schoolgirls defy the worst that Hitler can throw at them"; and when the All Clear sounded and we returned to our dormitory, it was not with any distress of what we might see from the uncurtained windows, but with a heartfelt prayer that the domestic science block had been razed to the ground. It never was, though the daylight raids brought the bliss of interrupted lessons, and an excuse for unfinished homework. Much later, when I was reunited with my friends who had stayed in London throughout the Blitz, I was astonished by how they vied for the top-dog experience, buried-under-debris pulling far greater rank than simply being bombed out.

If we sound an insensitive lot, there was good reason. Children are natural anarchists, and we who had been born between the wars had been all but broken on the treadmill of routine: potted at three weeks old, seldom picked up when we cried, stuffed to the gunnels with food whether we were hungry or not, and fed and bedded by the minute hand of an implacable clock. Is it any wonder that when our strait-jacketed life was literally blown asunder, we couldn't believe our luck? Then too, the sudden change in lifestyle was mirrored by a happy shift in the attitude of most adults who feared for our "nerves", and whose guilt at the dangers to which we'd been exposed drove them to overlook such major crimes as a grubby neck or an inability to change out of damp shoes. Above all, they actually grew quite matey, just as the whole of the country was learning to loosen up.

Imagine a typical suburban street, which had lived by the golden rule of "keeping itself to itself", suddenly being plunged into forming Warden and First Aid Posts, Savings Groups, Fire Watching teams, make-do-and-mend parties; and, when coal grew scarce, sharing the cooking and evening fires. No wonder that within weeks of continuous raids, communities were forged whose friendship and loyalty was so absolute that they not only survived the worst that the enemy could throw at them, but emerged with a faith in each other that was as unexpected as it was inspiring.

In this cynical and derisive age, it is impossible to convey the ideals and comradeship of that time without sounding downright sentimental. All I know is that the country stared at the map of Nazi Europe and saw that the only resistance was from a small island in the left-hand corner; an island that had been hopelessly unprepared, whose Army had been driven into the sea, and whose lifeline supplies were being blockaded by the German U-boats at sea. We were alone, and knew that it was literally sink into slavery, or resist and swim against a tide of Fascism that was hell-bent on destroying us.

Not that this was put into words, for it was the one reticence that was retained. As always, it was humour that helped people to dilute the enemy to the manageable size of a nursery nuisance. "Hitler's such a little fidget"; "I see we're frying tonight" as bombs exploded in all directions; and the favourite put-down when enemy flares pinpointed a target: "At least it's a good light to read by".

Except during the devastation of Coventry, the government's prediction of a mass exodus from the towns failed to materialize, though at the height of the bombing some made nightly treks to the safety and peace of the countryside. No. In general, people clung to their homes while they still had homes to cling to, for often they were all that remained of a pre-war world, though it was the odd domestic detail that most reassured when the occupants returned from the chaos beyond their own patch. Imagine leaving for work and discovering that your usual route had been put out of action, so you shunt yourself from one unknown bus to another, squashed together with the rest who've been bombed off their regular transport. Then, when you arrive at the office hours late, it's to find it has been flattened, and a warden tells you to get back home and await instructions.

Not easy when the new route you took has been blocked off because of a leaking gas main, and you have to trudge through a flood of burst water pipes, thumb a lift in a lorry and then walk two miles until, exhausted and filthy, you turn the corner and sigh with relief that at least your home is still standing. It is then that a familiar creaking gate reassures that life still holds *some* continuity.

Then, too, it was the small things that broke your heart. The sliced house exposing a nail holding a flannel; the fork protruding from a mountain of rubble; the burst pillow lying in the mud; and if one day you arrived home to find it gutted, it was a shattered pencil box that caused you to break down and cry. Yet even this had a gift in its bitter wake, for when it finally dawned that people and possessions were transitory, it was the abstracts that remained to comfort: friendships, endurance, and above all the *idea* of freedom, the *principles* of democracy.

Even at the death of a loved one, these gave some comfort, for at least they'd died for a cause; and when you followed the coffin to the graveyard, the lines of freshly covered graves bore witness to the belief that the living must continue to endure, if only for them. Not that, at the time, anyone knew how many thousands had been killed, for the numbers, especially those of any mass killings, were censored, and only seeped out in rumour: the direct hit on an underground station, when water and sewage poured through the fissures to drown the people beneath; or the hundreds who were squashed and suffocated when bomb blast threw travellers into an amorphous mass of wounded and dying at the bottom of a flight of steps.

Despite the many and terrible tragedies involving the underground, it was still considered the safest place during air raids. At the start of the Blitz, it was forbidden to use the underground as a shelter, and though public pressure soon reversed this decision, when they were first opened they were squalid and stinking sanctuaries. However, as the bombardment continued, regular users and the civilian Services set out to make them, if not a home from home, then the next best thing. Mesh bunks were installed on the platforms, together with chemical lavatories, First Aid posts, and trollies with tea urns or even canteens; while the truly houseproud stations produced their own magazines and entertainment, including amateur and professional performances of modern and classical plays, concerts, Christmas shows, films, evening classes, discussion groups, libraries and inter-platform darts. Gradually, the richness of life that had been so disrupted above the ground, re-established itself in the underworld beneath, and sometimes to even better effect, for those too poor to spare money for entertainment, could, for the first time in their lives, enjoy it for free.

Here's a typical evening. It's six o'clock. Mr Smith is on fire-watching duty at his office, but first he escorts his wife and two children down the immobilized escalators, all of them humping bags of food and drink, blankets, small toys, playing cards, face cream, curlers and damp flannels wrapped in towels. The Smiths have established No. 4 and 5 bunks on Platform 2 as their own, and though they're late, they know they'll be reserved by the Joneses and Browns who have bunks on either side. In the past few weeks they've all become very pally, and now share their food while exchanging news of what's happened in the already unreal world above their heads. As for the children, Tommy is showing Jim and Elizabeth a piece of shrapnel that landed in the bird-bath, while Susan joins her new friends in the playgroup at the end of the platform. Afterwards they'll have a snack and be put to bed, nose to tail in the top bunks. For the adults, there's a full evening, starting with a discussion group whose subject tonight is "Education in Post-War Britain", followed by Fred from First Aid on the accordion, ably assisted by Brenda on the washboard, and which will surely develop into a sing-song with Mrs Smith giving her usual rendering of "Some Day My Prince Will Come", and, what's more, with graphic gestures.

This programme, to a greater or lesser extent, was played out in all the larger stations, and which, like all gatherings, contained its own pecking order as well as its good souls and its bores: Mr X who drones on about the perfection of his last billet on Platform 3 in Aldgate East; Mrs Y who plans to take over the tea urn, and given a fair wind, the entire canteen; and watch out for Mr Z because whatever has befallen you, he'll go one worse; and when at last everyone has bedded down for the night, it's always little Miss A who can spare the last of the tea from her flask.

For those who failed to achieve the luxury of a bunk, it was the escalators, passages, platform floors or even, after the power was cut off, the filth of the lines themselves. But whatever the space, it was jealously guarded, and woe betide anyone who shifted their territory even an inch into someone else's. And thus, through the night, most of them slept. It was airless and smelly, they were squashed together and stepped over, snores trumpeted in the confined and echoing space, but at least it was almost safe. In the morning, those on the lines shifted first; and when the early trains stopped at the platform, the passengers were forced to pick their way over the late sleepers, who slowly gathered their things together and dragged themselves and their belongings up the endlesss stairs and into the carnage of the city above.

In every week of September 1940, 40,000–50,000 people were made homeless, either temporarily or permanently; on 15 October at the peak of the bombing, 538 tons of explosives were dropped; in November, 4,500 were killed, with many more wounded; and in December, the death toll in London alone was over 12,500, city life settling into a grim routine of long working hours, interrupted travel packed to suffocation, and continuous sleepless or broken nights. Grey with exhaustion, many emerged from the shelters to find their gas and electricity cut off, stand-pipes the only source of water, and candles beneath a homemade stand the only means of boiling a kettle or even cooking. And always and over everything lay a thick coating of dust. It seeped round loosened window frames and doors, between floorboards, through gaping roofs, into drawers and wardrobes, and even between protective sheets of tissue paper, until there rose from the cities the anguished cry: "I'll never be clean again". This was hardly helped when most nights were spent fully dressed, and when, in the public shelters, the only chance of washing was under a coat with a damp flannel, mothers instructing their children to do only the "important little places". And when, dirty, thirsty and fed up, people returned home to find the water cut off, they used the water in the firebucket, even if it was floating with part of the ceiling.

And yet people managed, and with a fierce humour that made light of all but the worst disasters. A partly demolished police station bore the endearing sign: "Be good — we're still open"; blasted shops carried signs in the window frames announcing "More Open Than Usual", or "Come inside — there's nothing to stop you"; and when there was a sale of bomb-damaged goods, it was "Prices sliced — just like us"!

Within a week of the bombing, the hated air raid warden had become a national hero, with his or her cheery shout of "We'll have you out in no time" to victims buried beneath the rubble, the continued and reassuring chatter blurring into the sound of moving masonry as Heavy Rescue dug down to a trapped citizen, or worst of all, a child too shocked to scream. And when at last the still-alive were pulled free with their mouths and noses blocked with filth, it was neighbours, passers-by, nurses, the WVS, the fire service and ambulance crews who rallied round to clean the victim and check for injuries, before helping numbed hands round a comforting mug of tea. Then, if the victims had lost their homes, they were helped to centres to be given food, clean clothes, personal effects, and even a bed until they could be temporarily housed. This was when the advanced planning and the legion of clerks came into their own: identity cards and ration books were issued, the Post Office informed, and, if broke, emergency funds handed out; and when at last the victim *was* housed, bits of essential furniture were donated and more-or-less normal life could begin again. These scenes were played out, night after night, day after day, until the winter weather brought bad flying conditions and a chance to catch up on sleep and to patch what was left of the cities and towns.

Here's our typical suburban street: a third of the windows damaged; tarpaulin over four roofs; Nos 13, 15 and 17 demolished, the surviving occupants living with the families at 37, 42, and over the corner shop whose window is boarded up except for a small pane of glass. Not that there is much to see, what with food rationing and the new cardboard packaging and dreary labels. At the intersection with the Crescent, the Water Board has installed a stand-pipe, but they've promised that the mains will be working by Christmas, so at least the street will be able to have a good wash, and not have to carry the water for cooking its hoarded rations for the Christmas dinner. As for the children, what with the school demolished and parents occupied with their war work, they're having a perfectly splendid time playing on the forbidden bomb sites, and, what's more, with grubby everything, because bath night is a thing of the past!

In contrast to the young, the old suffered dreadfully, many of them unable to get to the shelters, or preferring to take their chance amidst the familiar treasures of home. "If I'm going to snuff it, I'd rather go in my own bed" was the attitude, and who can blame them, when the cold of the shelters was just as likely to kill. Then, too, though the winter months brought a let-up in raids, there was so little fuel that they could hardly remember what it was like to be warm. Nevertheless, for many who'd lived out their retirement in isolation, the horror of the Blitz was tempered by a host of new and unlikely friends: air-raid wardens who checked after raids, the neighbour who refilled buckets of water, the woman from the WVS who insisted on providing an extra rug and explained that she'd get into trouble if the gift wasn't accepted. Then there were the tradesmen, with whom it would have been unthinkable to be friendly before the war, but who now shared the same tragedies and hopes, and to whom it would have been rude not to enquire if their families were safe. Above all, pride was rekindled when their talents were once more in demand: unravelling old jerseys and reknitting them, keeping an eye on the house opposite whose door no longer shuts, or babysitting while the mothers drove ambulances, fire-watched, or attended First Aid classes.

Thus, though the Christmas of 1940 was a frugal and makeshift celebration, the street enjoyed it together, proud of the community spirit that it had forged, and which would have been so unthinkable only a year earlier. What they could not have known, was that the nation's habit of shared responsibility must to some measure have paved the way for the acceptance of Beveridge's plan for post-war social security.

In the meantime, the enemy bombers continued to lay waste the cities and towns and villages, and to kill and injure thousands upon thousands of people; until, during a spate of short sharp raids in 1944, Churchill warned that there might soon be attacks by pilotless flying bombs and rockets. Not that the nation took much notice, for it was preoccupied with the coming invasion of Europe, and saw little point in worrying about something that might or might not happen.

On 6 June 1944, the Allies landed in France. A week later, the V1 bombs landed in Britain. Far more sinister because they were mechanical, aside from being shot down over open country or the sea, their interception was as dangerous as if they had reached their targets, for they exploded on impact. Nicknamed the Buzz Bomb because of the sound of the engine, the moment of terror was the sudden silence when it cut out and fell.

No one who lived through that bombardment will ever forget the desperate prayers that the engine wouldn't cut out but fly on, and the awful guilt that by definition one was willing the monster to kill somebody else. Also, there was the chilling knowledge that the second they were fired from their platforms, nothing could alter their given course. People would stop in the middle of a job as they pictured a distant finger pressing the button that would destroy them.

To give some idea of the V1 carnage, some fifteen years ago I wrote the following paragraph in my autobiography:

The explosion tore through the street. One moment I was buying a paper, holding out my penny to a rosy-cheeked newsvendor, and the next I was flat on my face, the papers hurtling over me as the world crumbled. The deafening blast spread like a tidal wave, lifting whole roofs and blowing the buildings outwards; and though it was only a matter of seconds they seemed to move in slow motion, walls of brick and glass sinking to their foundations like old women lowering themselves into chairs. Then, screams rose with the dust, the paper man lying in the gutter, his groin red and slippery as his fingers searched amongst the tatters of his trousers. Above me a woman lolled in a tree, her face stupid in death as she held her shopping basket; and a child leapt from a butcher's window clutching a leg of lamb drenched in his blood.

Once again, the government evacuated the children, and people fled to the safety of the country, though far fewer left than in '39, for many clung to the hope that the rocket bases would be captured by the Allies in their advance. "If Hitler thinks I'm budging now, then he's another think coming" was the general attitude. However, the "other thing coming" was to be over us.

On 8 September, V2 rockets devastated Chiswick in London, to be followed by others throughout the city, including one rocket on Deptford that killed 300 people. So terrible was this latest menace that despite the cheering news of the victories in Europe, the government censored all reports of the rockets on the ground that they would lower morale. Not that many were surprised when six weeks later Churchill finally told the nation, for rumours, like the rockets were unstoppable.

Yet again, in the fifth year of war, people gritted their teeth and somehow endured. Worn out, rationed to the barest minimum, often in makeshift accommodation, and without the comforting thought that the winter would bring respite, they kept on keeping on. Hardest of all to bear was the news that the Germans were starting to put up a stiff resistance, so that any dream of a Christmas at peace was doomed. Instead, it was back to the shelters and sleepless nights. Again the underground echoed to tramping feet, as the people returned with hardly enough energy to organize entertainments, let alone celebrate. Not that they didn't try, but the regulars were long gone, and the decorations that were put up seemed to enhance rather than cover the peeling paint and exposed concrete.

Only when the final rocket had fallen, and the last All Clear sounded, did the nation allow itself to admit the exhaustion that it had somehow managed to hide, even from itself. Pinched with fatigue, the people threw away their gas masks and blackout material, rolled up their sleeves, and began to clean up what was still standing.

*

The next time you pass an open car park, look up to see if the buildings on either side have been buttressed, or if their fascias seem to be slashed in half. If they are, then it is probably an old bomb site. And if you can spare a moment, give a thought to the people who had once lived there and sometimes died.

CHAPTER
FIVE

Food

It is a truth universally acknowledged that the British have never been inventive cooks. If this is so, then what the hell were we up to during the war, when potatoes were transformed into pastry, carrots into jam, and an unspeakable fish called snoek was so disguised that many managed to swallow it. No, the real truth is that the wartime dishes conjured from scraps by cooks, housewives and the Ministry of Food stood on a par with the miracle of the Loaves and Fishes; and though both were born of desperation, in Britain the hunger of many was not simply a one-off.

In 1937, malnutrition was so rampant amongst the poor that a survey of the capital's council schools revealed that 67 to 80 per cent of the children had bone disorders, 67 to 82 per cent suffered from enlarged or septic tonsils, and an unbelievable 88 to 93 per cent had malformed or decaying teeth; while in 1939, one in four were deemed to be undernourished, and this at a time when the country could afford to import 60 per cent of its food. Not that many appeared to be bothered overmuch, and it wasn't until the nation was forced to come face to face with hunger, that the statistics became pinched faces and stunted growth.

It was the government's evacuation of children that

finally forced a national outcry, when their hosts discovered that many refused to eat unfamiliar fruit and vegetables and demanded their usual fare of sausages, fish and chips, bread and scrape, and tea instead of milk. When a child is hungry and its parents have little money, it is quantity and not quality that counts; and though it seems a contradiction, it was the reduction in national food supplies that forced a more equal distribution of basic nourishment and brought to an end the malnutrition of so many.

As in other spheres, it was the advertisements that first indicated what was to become a revolution in our eating habits. As early as 29 September 1939, and under the heading "Egg Supply In War Time", the copy announced: "Learn how you can produce your own eggs cheaply. Follow the invaluable advice given in *The Feathered World*". Later, the government announced that it planned to reclaim a million and a half acres of derelict land for growing food, a declaration which, with the early issue of ration books, and rumours that the enemy planned to bomb warehouses, so stimulated a panic buying of food that it probably brought forward the rationing that so many dreaded.

Food rationing was introduced in the first month of 1940, with special needs identified by books with various coloured covers. Besides the basic 4 oz butter, ham and bacon, 3¼ oz cooked ham and 12 oz sugar, pregnant women were given first choice of oranges and bananas, a daily pint of milk and the right to jump the queue! Aside from the last privilege, children up to five received the same rations; while the fives to sixteens had half a pint of milk a day and extra fruit. For vegetarians, heavy manual and agricultural workers, there was extra cheese; and invalids and religious sects had modified rations according to their needs. So as to make sure that shops had enough stocks but were not over-supplied, everyone had to register with a single grocer, butcher and dairy, the unlooked-for consequence being the reversal of a time-honoured pecking order. No longer were shop assistants required to be obsequious to even the most difficult customer, for it was the shop that was now all powerful and the shopper who was dependent. Of course, everyone received their due rations, but who would settle for bits of bacon end when a "Please" and "Thank you" obtained Best Back. Indeed, as the war continued and unrationed goods grew scarce, some women even dressed up for the shopkeepers, their winsome smiles bringing the rest of the queue to boiling point, and the flinging of insults featuring the dubious morals of such unpatriotic and ingratiating behaviour.

A month after rationing began, meat was added, and of all the wielders of power, the butcher became paramount, for the ration did not include such delicacies as offal, liver, calves' and pigs' feet, sausages, hash, calves' head, melts and skirt. Standing like some high priest, knife poised in sceptre position behind his marble altar, the butcher was not only wooed with sweet words, but tickets to this and that, and much under-the-counter barter. For the lucky few that he chose to favour, an unknown "something" in a plain wrapper was surreptitiously slipped into the shopping basket, and not until the customer was well clear of the prying eyes of the queue was the content examined, and oh, the triumph if it was liver! Not that everyone asked for extras or even brought their whole ration, for though the price of rationed goods was controlled, it wasn't until 1943 and full employment that all could afford them.

This then was the beginning of rationing which was to

vary from month to month according to supplies. Rather than listing all the many additions and changes, here is the least and the most allowed per week:

Meat:	1 shilling to two and a pennyworth
Bacon:	4 oz – 8 oz
Cheese:	1 oz – 8 oz
Fat:	1 oz – 8 oz
Eggs:	½ – 2
Tea:	2 oz – 4 oz
Sugar:	8 oz – 16 oz + 2 lbs for jam-making
Sweets:	3 oz – 4 oz (including chocolate)
Dried Milk:	¼ tin
Dried eggs:	8th of a packet.

Later, other groceries in short supply were put on a "points" system which varied according to availability, and which included such items as tinned fish and fruit, beans and macaroni. In the end, there was very little, aside from seasonal fruit and vegetables, and for some time bread, that wasn't rationed. However, people put up with it because it was fair. Only Winston Churchill was exempt, for the Royal Family chose to share the same privations as their subjects, though one or two Members of Parliament voiced their concern at the thought of a minuscule chop on a gold plate!

From the start of the war, milk was in short supply because of a shift from dairy farming to crops, but because of the admirable policy that those most in need must — whatever their income — receive the most nutrients, milk for pregnant women and the under-fives was provided free if the family earnings were below £2 a week. Otherwise it was twopence a pint, though not necessarily in bottles, which soon became scarce, but ladled into a customer's jug. Extra school milk for the over-fives was a third of a pint, of which three-quarters was subsidized, while the poorest received it free. With school meals expanding from 250,000 to 1,850,000, it's little wonder that wartime children flourished, their newborn sisters and brothers growing strong on cod liver oil and orange or rosehip-syrup; and I well remember that when the American soldiers arrived, they were amazed at the rosy health of our babies.

But back to the beginning and the shopkeepers. Despite their new-found power, theirs was not a happy lot. Aside from being showered with directives and almost monthly changes, every rationed item was represented by a tiny square in the ration book that had to be cut out or cancelled before being counted, itemized on forms, and the whole lot sent to the local Food Office. This added hours to an already long working week; but though the extra work increased rather than diminished, the appointment of Lord Woolton as Minister of Food in the spring of 1940 did much to dampen a simmering revolt.

Despite having an almost impossible task, Lord Woolton became one of the most popular of all the war ministers. Indeed, he was loved, for not only was he efficient, having been head of the prosperous John Lewis shop in Manchester, but he possessed a rare degree of empathy born of his personality and years as a social worker. Above all, he had the wisdom never to lecture but to explain. It was these qualities, as well as his benign favourite-uncle smile, that helped us not only to accept every new privation, but to take a pride in the fact that ours was the most efficient distribution of food in the world. And what an innovator he was! First he launched "Food Facts" in the newspapers and magazines, explaining why such-and-such was in short supply, and giving helpful recipes for whatever food was featured for that day; then "Food Flashes" were introduced following the 8.15 a.m. news on the radio. Of course, like now, there were regular listeners who strongly objected to the innovations, and refused to listen to *any* advice aside from the Radio Doctor, who gave lovingly detailed descriptions of common complaints, plus helpful hints on how to keep listeners "regular". Indeed, Doctor Hill's lugubrious tone and flights of rhetoric brought the nation's obsession with its bowels to its peak, and it was no surprise when he became the head of the BBC some years later. After all, a man who can comprehend the tortured contortions of the British Inside will hardly be stumped by the Byzantine ramifications of Broadcasting House.

Aside from a theatrical delivery, the Radio Doctor stuck to the facts, whereas Lord Woolton sometimes flung them aside altogether, and devoted a whole item to our moral uplift.

> We go to training for the Finals. We harden ourselves and we discipline our lives. Only by fostering every ounce of our national resources — in our kitchen just as much as in our manufactures — can we field the team that will be unbeatable!
>
> Lord Woolton, Food Fact No.4

How could we resist such a minister, when he gave as much thought to our souls as to our bodies? He was our Food Front Churchill, who bade us go forth and bring back the bacon with all the fervour of frontline troops.

Aside from rationing homegrown food, Britain still needed to replace the 60 per cent that had been imported, and which was threatened by enemy U-boat submarines. Luckily, if the British are anything it is dedicated gardeners, and the "Dig for Victory" campaign was the most outstanding success of the war. Building on a long tradition of allotments and vegetables grown in back gardens, what more natural than that the population should set to and dig up every scrap of derelict land, together with road verges, golf courses, parks, school grounds, playing fields, and bomb sites? You name it, we dug it, mulched it, weeded it, hoed it and planted it, our cities and railway embankments burgeoning with cabbages, carrots, potatoes, onions, beetroots and leeks. Gardening clubs were formed to share tools and expertise, and to swap cuttings and seeds; and gangs of amateur farmers dug up lawns, or if they didn't have one, planted window-boxes. Town houses, whose window-sills had once sported elegant blooms, now grew lettuces and forests of tomatoes, so that the rooms within that had already been darkened by strips of paper criss-crossing the window-panes, now assumed a jungle gloom. Never mind, this was more than compensated for when the hostess could boast that *her* salad was homegrown and harvested with her own fair hands.

Having established Food Facts and Flashes, Lord Woolton then added the cartoon characters Potato Pete and Doctor Carrot to his advertisements. "Eat us," they cried, in the same vein as the pills that tempted Alice in her Wonderland; and indeed the propaganda that if we ate enough carrots we'd be able to see in the blackout was as much a fantasy as anything dreamed up by Lewis Carroll, for we would have had to gorge ourselves silly to make the slightest difference. Still, it all helped to cut down imports, and children who had refused to eat any raw vegetables now took to an endless munching of carrots, in the belief that when they grew up their X-ray eyes would allow them to join the pilot heroes who flew by night.

One of the most entrancing sights of the war was the flocks of sheep that grazed in the parks and commons; plus the rabbits, goats, chickens and pigs kept by individuals and cooperatives. Pig Clubs were particularly popular with fire stations and wardens' posts, the sow becoming a cherished member of the crew; and when she gave birth to a litter, it was looked on as a personal triumph not only by her solicitous attendants, but by the many outworkers who collected scraps, withstood the dreadful stink of boiling it into swill, and then carted the lot to the makeshift stye. Once, when I was taking a shortcut across a bomb site in the blackout, I overheard an unseen man whispering sweet nothings to his beloved. At that moment the moon appeared, and I saw that the paramour was not a girl but a truly gargantuan pig. Such treasures were always given a name, the jolly-hockey-sticks variety being especially favoured, and you learnt, on overhearing someone mention that Brenda now weighed over fifteen stone, that she was not necessarily some Junoesque woman. By the end of the war, 210,000 pigs had been fed by 31,000 tons of scraps collected by housewives and children.

Just as adults were exhorted to dig for victory, so schools, Brownies and cubs were press-ganged into collecting nuts, berries of all kinds, crab apples, quinces, wild mushrooms and hips. So successful were the children, that in 1943 they collected half a million tons of rosehips, which made enough syrup for every single baby in the country. I was one of these harvesters, albeit under duress. Every autumn weekend, groups from school fanned out over North Devon, ploughing up hill and down dale, drenched or burnt by the sun, and bitten by every insect known to our biology mistress. Stained like Ancient Britons due to steady sampling, we picked for hours, our backs breaking in the search for the tiny bilberries hidden at ground level, and which the school cook made into jam.

Deprived of sweet things, jam was one of the few luxuries left, and the Ministry of Food encouraged the nation to augment its ration by issuing an extra two pounds of sugar at harvest time. The recipes for homemade jam came in two strengths: weak, meaning runny but using the minimum sugar, and which had to be eaten within two months before it became mouldy; and the real McCoy that lasted as long as greed would allow. Official jam-making centres were set up, including one in my aunts' kitchen, neither of whom had had much to do with the culinary arts, but who viewed the operation as their patriotic duty. In the end, other and experienced cooks prevailed upon them to take over the paperwork, for the official jam had to be labelled with the day and place where it was made and at which "boil"; Aunt Grace, the book reviewer, writing the labels, and Aunt Pam, the motor mechanic, licking and slapping them on.

Because fruit was in such short supply, vegetables were added to plump out the mixture, carrots, swedes and marrows being particularly suitable. Not that anyone minded, because we'd all become used to any plentiful foodstuff, especially potatoes, being shoved into the most unlikely dishes. Month after month, and year after year, "Food Facts" hammered home the virtues of the British spud. It was homegrown, full of nourishment — especially under the skin so it mustn't be peeled unless necessary — and above all it was a filler.

> Dearly beloved brethren,
> Is it not a sin,
> To peel potatoes and to throw away the skin.
> The skin feeds the pigs
> And the pigs feed us.
> Dearly beloved brethren, is it not thus?

Potatoes were popped into pastry, rissoles, puddings, sandwiches and even cakes, where they joined the ubiquitous carrot which was used to sweeten. Not that many of these cakes would be termed such now, what with no-fat cakes, no-sugar cakes, and certainly no tasting-like-cake cakes. As for decoration, a covering of icing sugar or ordinary sugar sprinkled on shop cakes was banned; and marzipan was a word that covered such exotic mixtures as haricot beans, ground rice, a smidge of sugar, almond essence and margarine, and which according to Aunt Pam tasted of engine oil. Indeed, the taste of most traditional dishes suffered such a sea change that newspapers and magazines cautioned cooks that it might be as well not to mention the ingredients before eating them. They were told to smile when serving, and to talk about anything other than food until it was consumed. Not that there was much criticism, because it was a miracle that anyone managed to stretch the rations to a full week, let alone provide enough to leave the eater satisfied. Even so, the longing for a taste of the long-gone lemon was so strong, that Servicemen and women back from warmer climes produced them as the gift above rubies, the recipients literally drooling with saliva as they sniffed the beautiful yellow skin. Even a painting of a lemon had the same effect, and I remember swallowing hard as I gazed at a Dutch masterpiece featuring an overflowing bowl of fruit, from which the top of a single lemon leered out at my longing.

In the spring of 1941, enemy U-boats sank 700,000 tons of British shipping, and rationing really began to bite. Cheese was cut to 1 oz a week, and queues for off-ration food became so long and with so little at the end of them, that black market and luxury goods were at a premium. Not that any except the rich could afford some of the items, for a melon cost as much as many a weekly wage; and despite hunger, it was only a small minority who shopped on the black market. In an increasingly selfish age, the discipline of those under siege must seem too good to be true, but it was true, for everyone knew that having more than the ration meant that extra had to be imported, and with the mounting shipping losses, more food equalled more men lost at sea.

By the summer of '41, our plight was desperate. At one point, Lord Woolton stood on the heights of Hampstead Heath and looked down on London and despaired. Below him lay a city whose citizens were struggling to live amidst the squalor of bombardment, broken water mains and the pall of dust, unaware that an even greater peril threatened: unless our ships managed to break through the blockade, in two weeks there would be no rations. It was that close. But convoys of shipping did get through, and the debt that we owed to the Merchant Navy can never be over-estimated. Looked on as the lesser service compared with the Royal Navy, it was their courage and tenacity in the face of unbelievable odds that kept the last fighting democracy in Europe from starving.

In the autumn of that year, office workers were asked to help with the harvest, and land clubs were formed. Despite lack of sleep and lengthening working hours, in the evenings and at weekends they changed into old clothes, met at assembly points and were driven to farms to work until dark. Schools were roped in, children giving up part of their summer holidays to help gather the crops, my own school lifting potatoes on a farm in Slimbridge. We slept in tents on straw palliasses, and were fed by Italian prisoners of war who sang as they dished out the meals. It was hard work and a great adventure, and only marred by the arrival of a Ministry of Information film unit. Much to our indignation, they insisted on importing boys so as to film us playing off-duty cricket, whereas we were far too exhausted to do anything except read or write letters home. When I did get home, I was so infested with fleas that my mother insisted I got into the bath fully clothed, and I used up a whole month's ration of 4 oz of soap before I was clean. Still, it was all in a good cause, because the country had such a bumper crop of potatoes that the government ordered them to be sold at a penny a pound so that we would eat even more.

It was during 1941 that people began to barter in earnest. Here's our typical suburban street: Mr Brown at Number 54 specializes in growing beetroot, which he exchanges for cabbages from Number 18, who has such a surplus that he gives them to the old woman who's still keeping an eye on the rickety front door across the road. To repay him she darns his socks, as well as Mr Smith's at Number 5, who rewards her with tomatoes. The corner shop, which is having some difficulty in getting vegetables because the local railway station has been bombed, is now buying up any surplus from the four streets that meet at its corner, the children collecting the produce. Making the best of a tragedy, the gardens of the houses that were demolished during the Blitz are now farmed by a street co-operative; and the wardens' post keeps Elsie, the pig, in the shell of what was once Mrs Robinson's kitchen. With any luck, Elsie will reach the statutory weight for killing before Christmas, though I fear that if she doesn't make it she'll probably have an "accident", meeting her Maker in the blackout when the Law is busy somewhere else.

A mile from our street, a barter market has been established, and Mr Jones takes his surplus lettuces there, where he can exchange them for a greater variety of goods. He bicycles over very early in the morning, because if the corner shop finds out you can be sure his cheese ration will be mostly rind. Sad to say, Mrs Wright at Number 2 is keeping her precious onions to herself, and there's a rumour that she takes them up to Knightsbridge to sell on the black market. She has even refused to donate a single onion to the church fête, where the vicar could auction it for as much as £1. Her excuse is that the crop is diseased, but as Mr Smith remarked, "Not half as much as her conscience". One thing's for sure, she won't be asked to the Smiths' Christmas dinner. Despite a shortage of containers, Mrs Smith has begged and borrowed a dozen and is bottling like mad, and she's planning to make a Christmas pudding from a recipe without eggs: mix 1 cup of flour, breadcrumbs, sugar, mixed dried fruit — meaning a few raisins — and ½ cup of suet. Add 1 cup of grated potato and another of grated carrot, plus a teaspoon of bicarbonate of soda dissolved in two tablespoons of hot milk. Like last year, there are very few turkeys, and unless Elsie turns up her trotters, they'll have to make do with a week's ration of meat augmented with a stuffing of breadcrumbs and herbs from the bomb site. Still, the room'll look festive, for apart from the last of the pre-war decorations and the twigs dipped in whitewash, the magazines have supplied lots of helpful hints. "Greenery can be dipped in a solution of Epsom Salts to give frosting", and though there are "no gay bowls of fruit, vegetables have such jolly colours. The cheerful glow of carrots, the rich crimson of beetroot, the emerald of parsley — it looks as delightful as it tastes!" Sadly, Mr Smith, who isn't a regular at the pub or the off-licence, is finding such difficulty in buying alcohol that the little they have will be kept for the New Year, and may it be easier than this one!

But it wasn't. In February, soap was cut to 3 oz a month; then white bread was replaced by the National Loaf, which, though unpopular because of its grey hue and gritty texture, was much more nourishing because it contained most of the grain. And so the cuts went on, and not just food, but fuel, anything made of glass, razor blades and much much else. Then, and worst of all, milk was cut to 2½ pints a week, so that tea, which some were already calling gnat's pee, became a travesty of its robust pre-war self. One of the most depressing slogans of the Ministry of Food was "None for the pot", though many chose to brew the pre-war strength and then boil up the tea leaves for a second or even a third pot. Even so, when people visited, they often took a few tea leaves in a screw of paper, handing it to the hostess with a muttered "Thought this might help". And when Christmas came, people did

the best they could, using the last of their precious stores
in a desperate bid to make the day special.

Most people had a store cupboard of hoarded tins for the
very special occasion: someone's leave, the birth of a baby,
or that moment when life seemed so desperate that "Let's
live today because tomorrow we might be dead" seemed
the only sensible philosophy. My grandmother, who was
both ruthless and a sixty-eight-year-old flirt, had managed
to scrounge such mouth-watering stores that her cupboard
was christened Fortnum & Mason. Only very favoured
guests were allowed a sight of it, the door opened with
such tantalizing reverence that it might have been a holy
shrine. The pilgrims were not disappointed. In pride of
place stood a gigantic tin of ham, the picture of its contents
so succulent that many could hardly bear to look at it. "If
Harry is taken from me by that dreadful little Hitler, it'll
have top billing at his funeral luncheon," my grandmother
would announce, beaming down on grandfather as if this
was the ultimate proof of her devotion. He died a year
later, and not one of the family was able to swallow a
mouthful.

For the more joyous occasion of a wedding breakfast,
shops hired out a cardboard cake decorated with chalk
icing sugar, the real and much smaller cake nestling
underneath, and never enough to go round. Still, "Must
keep up appearances", or so we told ourselves, for luxury
food was so long gone that we only remembered it
in our dreams, or gazing into a shop window stacked
with cardboard facsimiles: dusty slabs of fruit-and-nut
chocolate, pre-war tins of painted toffees, and fading
cut-outs of walnut creams being popped in the rosebud
mouth of some gorging beauty.

And so our rationed lives continued: less here and a bit more there. 1944, and those over seventy were given a whole extra ounce of tea for Christmas; 1945, and the fish shops offered whale meat and the unspeakable snoek which was actually barracuda. Not that most of us didn't manage to eat the stuff, just as we'd eaten horse meat and been grateful for it.

However fair the rationing was, inevitably those with enough money managed to fare better. For one thing, they could eat in restaurants where the food was unrationed, albeit with a limited price for the meal and only one dish containing protein. Much cheaper were the government British restaurants started during the Blitz to feed the homeless, and which by 1944 served half a million meals a day. Many were housed in schools because of their kitchens, and there was one in Chelsea that was a favourite meeting place for writers and artists. The food stood on trestle-tables, served by motherly women in white turbans and overalls, who took a personal interest in their customers' work. "And how's that picture shaping up?" they'd bellow, as a disreputable figure flung himself through the door, with a muttered "Don't ask!" But they pressed on regardless, and with such sympathy that the artist was cajoled into finishing it, in gratitude christening them The Muses.

This then was how Britain managed to feed itself, the Ministry of Food alternating between moralizing and congratulating in the endless slogans: "Thoughtful shopping saves shipping"; "Turn over a new leaf, eat vegetables daily"; "Cargos cost lives, bread costs ships"; "Food or munitions. Eat potatoes instead".

It was at the beginning of 1945, during the liberation of Europe, that an extraordinary act of self-rationing took place. News had started to filter through that millions on the mainland were starving. Photographs appeared in the newspapers: scarecrow children surviving on under 500 calories a day; the old, their necks poking out of enormous collars that had once fitted, grubbing in dustbins for scraps; and mothers offering themselves for the currency of a few cigarettes so as to feed their families. It was not a government decision but the outcry of the people that forced it to send *all* the reserved stocks of food to the Continent. Belts were tightened yet again, as Britain lived off what it could harvest or slaughter. Cheese was cut, and powdered milk and rice disappeared, for these were foods that could be easily digested by shrunken stomachs. To the background of V2 rockets devastating pick-up points and the ports, ships were loaded in record time, while others arriving with food were redirected across the Channel. News of this compassionate armada travelled before it, and the hungry gathered at the ports watching in silence for the first hazy outline of a funnel. And when the ships docked and were unloaded, the crowds pressed forward to help carry the cargo to a waiting transport of prams, carts and bicycles, many cradling sacks in their arms as tenderly as if they were newborn babies.

Rationing ended nine years later.

CHAPTER
SIX

Men

In 1939, in a Britain with a far smaller population than now, over a million and a half men were unemployed, some so debilitated that they would fail the Services' medical, or scrape through into the lowest category. Many were shorter than average, had bad teeth or no teeth at all, and chronic diseases of the lung, including tuberculosis which was then a killer.

As a child I would see them from the top of the bus as it drove through a slum. Compared to my uncles, they seemed to be another species. They were ageless, or rather they all appeared to be old, with greasy caps, jackets buffed to a shine across the shoulders, and trousers frayed above shoes whose soles flapped like starving mouths. But it was the faces that made them so particularly alien: skin almost grey, cheeks pasted to the bone, and eyes so sunken that it was as if they were peering out of a mask. Even the way they stood was different: shoulders dragged forward and bent, hands dug into pockets, and often propped against a wall as if the very act of keeping upright was too exhausting. Mostly, they stood in tight groups for protection, though outside the Labour Exchange and soup kitchen their queues were so long that they disappeared around corners. But wherever they were, and whatever they were doing, they exuded defeat. And why not? Some had been out of work and near starvation for as much as a decade, or were so young that they'd known nothing except privation and a Means Test so severe that families were forced to keep them if just one was working.

Sometimes they'd venture into the more prosperous districts looking for jobs, and if they passed two smartly dressed people walking abreast, they'd step into the gutter and touch their caps. Nobody remarked on this, for the class system was so rigid that it seemed to be perfectly natural. But it wasn't, or why did a very ordinary child remember it so clearly and with such pain? Just as I remember the old soldiers pretending to be a band, their instruments no more than paper over a comb, or a battered mouth organ that had seen them through the hell of the trenches. On the monotone of their clothes, medals flashed like fool's gold beside homemade notices: "Wife and three kids", "Four years fighting for King and Country", "Please give to a man who has lost everything".

These then were some of the men who prayed that there wouldn't be another war. Yet it was the war that, if it didn't kill them, would take them out of the dole queue.

Between the spring of 1939 and the autumn of 1941, all eligible males between the ages of eighteen and fifty-two were conscripted, and the vast sump of the unemployed began to be drained. Many went into the Services, while those rejected, the too young, the too old, and conscientious objectors, found jobs in Civil Defence, the Fire Service, the newly formed ministries, and in positions vacated by the Servicemen. Even thousands of men in jail were released for war work; and for those already retired, or who had to stay at home because of family commitments, there was part-time work, the Observer Corps, and the Local Defence Volunteers, later renamed the Home Guard, and which was the first citizens' army since the Napoleonic threat of invasion in 1803.

On 22 May 1940, when our army was being pushed onto the beaches of Dunkirk, and there was a real threat of invasion, the passing of the Emergency Powers Act gave a desperate government almost unlimited power over people and property. From then on, adult civilians could be required to do anything, and, furthermore, be sent anywhere; for with the bombing of cities and ports, firms and factories were still evacuating to places of safety.

In the factories, working hours were extended until many worked an eighty-hour week, and for those directly involved in Defence, a twelve-hour day, six days a week was statutory, while the aircraft industry worked a ten-hour day, seven days a week. The conditions were often horrendous. Denied daylight and air, because high windows couldn't be curtained and had to be shut and covered in black paint, workers spent their shifts in noisy, badly lit and stuffy workplaces, that could be sweltering in summer and freezing in winter; while some continued to work after an air raid alert, only downing tools when a roof spotter sighted enemy planes. Even then it was not unusual to don a tin hat and continue. Given the working conditions on top of often long journeys to and from overcrowded billets, it's small wonder that the government was concerned about the workers' well-being when it could lead to a fall in production. Canteens and rest-rooms were opened, regular health checks instigated, and to counteract the monotony of endless hours doing repetitive jobs, the BBC broadcasts of "Music While You Work" were relayed to the factory floor. Even lunch hours were enhanced by concerts and entertainment, and in the larger factories, a hairdresser was provided on the premises. However, despite all efforts, conditions and hours were sometimes so intolerable that workers were driven to strike, even though it was illegal and could carry a prison sentence. Such "unpatriotic" behaviour was kept from the public, on the grounds that it was defeatist and would undermine morale.

Of all the industries, the miners had more cause than anyone to strike, for conditions had hardly changed since the First World War, and pits were seriously undermanned due to the government's stop-go policy. Though mining had been a reserved occupation, after the Nazis overran Europe and we lost our overseas markets for coal, Britain had such large stocks that it was no longer deemed a Reserved Occupation for miners under thirty. Thousands were called up, while thousands more who had suffered the privations of part-time work during the slump volunteered for the Services or joined the expanding workforce in the factories. A year later, coal stocks had become so low that any under-thirties left in the pits were forbidden to leave, and the Army released 33,000 ex-miners who were forced to return to their old job. Despite this, there was still a shortfall of over 80,000 men and millions of tons of coal. From then on, and because supplies to industry could not be cut, fuel was rationed to all domestic consumers. Even so, the need for coal was so dire that in 1942 any man could opt for the mines rather than being called up. Few chose to do so; and in 1943, the position was so desperate that sixth-form schoolboys were asked to volunteer, but even an appeal to the idealistic young met with little response. Finally, a percentage of each new call-up of eighteen-year-olds was directed to the mines, though the scheme was so unpopular that many chose to be sent to jail instead. The boys who did become miners were nicknamed Bevin Boys after the Minister of Labour, and I remember some of them when I was stationed at an ATS training camp in Pontefract. Looking more like children than men, they would sit in the corner of a pub, ostracized by the professional miners who jeeringly referred to them as Mummy's Boys or Little Lord Fauntleroys. Happily, men were in such short supply around our camp that the ATS had no such prejudice, and many a lonesome lad was only too grateful to be taught the facts of life by a girl in khaki.

While the younger civilians were forced to work where they were directed, the elderly and old were asked to volunteer. In the BBC television series *Dad's Army*, a motley crew of mostly old men trained to repel the Nazi invaders, and though their characters and antics were heightened for comedy, it was in many ways a true presentation of the Home Guard. That said, I know that if there *had* been an invasion, their courage in defence of their country would have been heroic. Many had fought in the First World War, had returned home to what they believed would be a lifetime of peace, and then, while enjoying a retirement doing nothing more strenuous than getting on with their hobbies, they were asked to serve yet again. Their response to the call was immediate and they volunteered in their thousands, only to become the butt of jokes when they drilled with broom handles before there were enough rifles to go round. But old men are stoical, and they continued to drill despite the catcalls of small boys, the so-called gentle send-up of comedians, and endless cartoons in the press.

To a catchphrase of "Take one with you" if they were confronted by the enemy, they trained and became expert in putting up road blocks and barbed wire; making bombs; identifying enemy personnel, aircraft and equipment; mastering the Lewis and Vickers guns, the automatic rifle and hand grenades. In defence of our villages and towns, they patrolled day and night and in all weather until the threat of invasion had passed, when they assisted any organization that requested their services. They were a splendid band of men; and when they formed the guard of honour on Armistice Day and during Victory Week, their pride in their uniform was more than reflected in those who cheered them.

The highspot of Home Guard training was a simulated invasion, in which one company attempted to capture another company's territory. Uncle Bobby, whose monocle fell from his eye when startled, and who spattered his talk with the native slang he'd picked up during service in Malaya, was head of the Home Guard in a town that had to be held against "Enemy" attack, the enemy being a despised company in a nearby village, whose commander was known to the family as "the rotter who once made eyes at your sainted Aunt". As it was the school holidays, I was roped in as his personal messenger; and oh, what a perfectly splendid time we both had, for while I'm told that my uncle was highly efficient, he did rather play to the gallery, meaning me. Sitting in his hut HQ at a wonky card-table groaning under Important and Secret Papers, he would issue orders in that staccato English favoured by film stars in wartime epics. "Cut along to Smithers. Pick up the gen," he'd bark, and I'd plonk a tin hat on my head that was interwoven with a camouflage of dying leaves, before crawling via undergrowth to an even smaller hut, where the Second-in-Command was manning a field telephone. Here I'd be handed more secrets, which I was instructed to conceal about my person, before returning on hands and knees to the HQ.

Throughout the day we fought long and hard, Uncle Bobby refreshing himself from a hip flask that had done sterling service "Up Country", and which was referred to as "me other half". It was late afternoon when the enemy burst in upon our fastness and shouted "Hands up", Uncle Bobby's monocle leaping out of its socket as if he'd been shot. However the "shooting" came later. The captured forces were marched to the town hall, where we were lined up in front of a balcony from which the Rotter surveyed our humiliation with smug satisfaction. Reading from a pretend Nazi directive, he announced that the town was now under his command, that we must all obey his orders, and that the leaders of the resistance would be shot. As Uncle Bobby was led away, he glanced upwards and announced in ringing tones that if only it had been the Real Thing, he'd have made damned sure he'd have taken one with him! A few days later, all who had taken part were congratulated, and though my uncle made a brave show of not giving a hoot, he went to some lengths never to visit the despised village again, even after peace had been declared in the rest of the country.

After the Home Guard was disbanded, many looked back on it as the highspot of their retirement. Like old soldiers everywhere, they'd gather in pubs to relive old battles and argue the finer points of tactics, but generally end with the declaration that if Hitler had dared to invade, they'd have given him as good as they got! And they would.

To return to the outbreak of war, and the men who were called up or volunteered: those who had passed their medical reported to training camps, and it was here, and sometimes for the first time, that their eyes were tested, their teeth cleaned, filled or extracted, and minor ailments cleared up or stabilized. The improvement in their health, plus three meals a day and endless physical training, changed many beyond recognition. Time and again, wives and mothers would exclaim: "I hardly recognize him, he's grown so, and he's got such muscles he can't get into his civvies." And faces changed too. Men who'd grubbed a living in smokey towns now lost their pallor and became ruddy from constant fresh air; while the drill sergeant who'd straightened their backs and forced them to stride out unwittingly instilled a new confidence that showed in their eyes and the set of their head. But then, imagine how it must feel after years of struggle, when not only the recruit had board and lodgings and regular pay, but his dependants received a small family allowance. On their first leave, most returned to a hero's welcome, to be cossetted by loved ones dressed in their best clothes and on their very best behaviour. It must have been wonderful, and though it didn't happen to everyone, it was enough to be remarked upon. For later recruits who lived in built-up areas, homecomings were very different, for there was always the fearful knowledge that for the first time in any war, more civilians than Service personnel were being killed. Indeed, it wasn't until the autumn of 1942 that deaths in the Services outstripped the civilians.

I saw one of these Servicemen. The street must have been bombed hours earlier, for the dust had settled, and there were no homeless sitting in the rubble with the blank stare of those who daren't think. It was unnaturally quiet except for the sound of bricks falling, and as I turned the corner I saw a soldier digging frantically at a mound that had once been a house. He was young and ginger-haired, with bleeding hands and boots slipping as he hurled brick after brick into the road. A woman appeared, and ran towards him shouting that no one was there. He took no notice. Later, she told me that his wife and two children had been taken to the mortuary, that because they had been burnt beyond recognition, he'd refused to believe they were all that remained of his family. The last I saw of him he was still digging, the woman waiting patiently, arms crossed and staring at the ground, until he was exhausted and needed comfort.

In our typical suburban street, it's 1943. The airman son of the couple who run the corner shop has been invalided out of the Air Force. He was badly burnt in the Battle of Britain, and after over a year in hospital, eleven operations, and a plastic surgeon rebuilding his face, he's come back home. At first he was too self-conscious to serve in the shop, but now everyone's used to the shiny pink skin and the new eyelid that doesn't quite shut. Even the Brown boy at Number 54 who'd screamed when he first saw him doesn't bother any longer, and at least the man's fiancée has stood by him, unlike some. The old woman who's still watching the door opposite, though it's been repaired and can now lock, has taken in the widow and small son whose father was killed in the desert, and who once lived at Number 24. They're company for each other, and the old woman minds the boy while his mother works in a factory. They say it takes her mind off her loss. Mrs Summers, who once had two boys in the Navy, has had the first postcard from her husband in a prisoner-of-war camp in Singapore. She's taken to going up to the West End in the evening, and somebody's been giving her nylon stockings. Mrs Wright, who's extended her black-marketeering to clothing coupons, says Mrs Summers has been getting the stockings from her, but nobody believes it and thinks she's just being kind. All together, the street's lost five civilian men; two in the Army; four in the Navy and Merchant Navy; one in the Air Force; plus one reported missing believed killed.

Now, it's 1945 and VE day. The street's having a party for the children and they've carried out tables and chairs, and everyone's contributed part of their rations and what remains of the store cupboards. What with Mr Brown's beetroot and lettuces, Mrs Smith's bottled plums, and Mrs Wright's ask-no-questions-and-you'll-be-told-no-lies two pounds of chocolates, it's quite a feast and the children have gone beserk. They've even managed to bring out the piano of the old woman who's now bedridden, and the milkman at No. 3 is playing it fit to bust. Many of the street's Servicemen have already been discharged and some are wearing the demob suits that were issued free when they handed in their uniforms. The rest wouldn't be seen dead in them, and Mrs Wright has snapped them up for a song and re-sold them to a second-hand clothes shop in Tottenham Court Road. Everyone's smiling and talking their heads off, but if you look closely, you'll notice the lines of exhaustion, and the blank eyes of those whose sons and husbands and fathers are buried in the four corners of the earth. But we mustn't mention them because this is a party, and even the granddaughter of Elsie the pig has a bow round her neck.

Tomorrow the men will start thinking about the future

and wondering if they'll get their old jobs back; and though they've nothing but praise for the women who took them over, it's only fair that they should return to their proper place in the home.

CHAPTER SEVEN

Women

Democracy: "Government by the *majority*, by direct or representative rule". "Society characterized by recognition of equality of rights and privileges."

In 1918, Britain ceased to be ruled by a minority and became a democracy, when women of thirty and over were given the vote. Only in 1928, eleven years before the outbreak of war, did women achieve parity with men when they could vote at twenty-one. Thus, the first time that Britain fought to defend its democracy, was the war of 1939-45.

To show some of the enormous changes and opportunities that the war brought to women, it is necessary to know something of their lives in pre-war Britain.

The arena for women set by Hitler — "kitchen, nursery and church" — was, and only to a slightly lesser extent, reflected in the rest of Europe, where the proper role for women was seen to be as wives and mothers. If proof is needed, British spinsters and widows who outnumbered bachelors were referred to as "surplus". While the majority of the older "surplus" struggled to survive in low-paid jobs and on investments and pensions, how the young passed their time between school and their fathers giving them away into the safe-keeping of a bridegroom, was dictated by money and class. Daughters of prosperous parents were expected to stay at home and enjoy themselves or help their mothers; those of poorer families "filled in" by working in usually dead-end jobs, while only the very poor continued to work after achieving the longed-for status of wife. Indeed it was a husband's proud boast that *his* wife stayed at home, and that he would never permit her to work.

Given that most parents expected their daughters to marry, and that it was held that men disliked brainy women, it was thought a waste of time and money for a girl to receive a higher education, even if she was clever. Most accepted this, and the few who were determined to enter a profession had to fight for it, for unless a daughter obtained a scholarship, a university education depended on her father's willingness to pay. To add to the difficulties, there were so few university places for girls, that unlike boys who only needed a certificate of matriculation, a girl needed to study for a further *two* years before she could sit the stiff entrance examination. Even then, if she wished to become a doctor, medical schools' quotas were only 10 per cent, and some refused to accept them at all; while Cambridge did not award women degrees, whatever the subject, until the late forties. Before this they received a paper stating that they were educated up to degree standard.

If, at last, a woman did achieve her chosen qualifications, many professions were hedged with restrictive rules, for with unemployment increasing throughout the late twenties and early thirties, it became government *policy*, rather than ancient practice, to bar married women from teaching, working in government departments, and in hospitals and clinics as nurses or doctors; while many other professions and even offices so frowned on a woman continuing in her job after marriage that she was forced to resign.

For the majority of less privileged girls who left school at fourteen in order to contribute to the family income, the choice of employment was limited, promotion rare, and wages far less than men doing equivalent jobs. Most of these girls worked in light industry, hospitals, shops, offices and as servants.

To be a servant in the thirties was to be a drudge, working from dawn to dusk at the very least, and for a minimum wage. Time off was a half-day, Sunday after washing up the breakfast, and two evenings a week; and if she had a "follower" he was vetted for suitability, and she was not allowed to entertain him in the house. A domestic had to come and go by the tradesmen's entrance, and even when she was off-duty, she was expected to dress "according to her station". This meant that if she aped her "betters" by wearing glamorous clothes and frivolous hats, she was considered "fast" and given the sack. With so many restrictions, plus long hours of never-ending work, it's little wonder that girls preferred the expanding light industries, and that servants became difficult to find. This was referred to as "the servant problem" rather than the mistress's fault, and a friend of my mother's who'd housed her maid in a glorified passage between the kitchen and dining-room, was so incensed when she left that she stated that without the orphanages, family life would cease to exist. But there *were* orphanages, where girls had no choice but to train as nurses if they were very bright, and domestics if they weren't, and where they were raised in the discipline of obedience without question. Most had an air of subjugation, pale and spotty faces from inadequate feeding, and rough and swollen hands from years of scrubbing and working in the laundry. To my eternal shame, and though I was only a year or two younger, it never crossed my mind to talk to an orphan maid who worked for my aunt, nor I'm sure did she expect it, for we had both been raised within the strictures of class in which the Good Lord had seen fit to place us.

> The rich man in his castle,
> The poor man at his gate,
> He made them high and lowly,
> And ordered their estate.

So there we all were, boxed in by birth, money, education and prejudice. We lived in a world where girls were brought up to please, kept in ignorance of sex, and advised not to win when competing with boys. And when we grew up, birth control was difficult to come by and somehow dirty; abortion was a criminal offence; respectable restaurants refused to serve us in the evening if we were unaccompanied; it was shameful to enter a pub; and no one, including the police, must ever interfere between a husband and wife, even if she was being beaten. We were the homemakers, the keepers of the nation's morals, the little women and the weaker sex.

And then came the war.

By September 1939, millions of women had joined the many voluntary organizations, including the WVS which was to become the backbone of help for the civilian population. They trained in First Aid and joined the Red Cross and St John's Ambulance Corps; the Civil Defence in preparation for air raids; the women's Armed Services; the Land Army and the nursing organizations.

At home and on top of their usual chores, they prepared their children for evacuation or volunteered to take in evacuees, packed for and took over the responsibilities of husbands, brothers, sons and fathers who had been called up, made blackout curtains and painted skylights, filled buckets with water and earth, and learnt how to use a stirrup pump in case of fire.

Determined to do more, they tried to find part-time and full-time war work, but the government was loath to recognize that women's contribution would be essential to victory, and the Ministry of Information announced that unless a woman had special qualifications, and few had, she should stay in her peacetime job, or remain at home. After all, they reasoned, women were already giving service of national importance by caring for the nine million children under fourteen — no plans for nursery schools yet, by caring for the six million old people, and the millions of war workers and evacuees. In other words, women's best contribution was as handmaidens to dependants, and housekeepers to those making a direct contribution to the war effort.

However, nothing changes attitudes faster than need, and after seven and a half million of the nation's youngest and healthiest men had joined the Services, and with more anticipated, it became clear that women would *have* to replace them. Not that some of the vacant jobs weren't considered unsuitable, and this despite the fact that women had worked on the railways, in ammunition factories and as ambulance drivers during the First World War.

It was during 1940 when the Nazis overran Europe, and the unthinkable was only too possible, that any lingering doubts died, and the government actively began to recruit women into the workforce. Like the men, they worked anything from a fifty-seven- to an eighty-hour week, which rose to an unbelievable 112 hours in the aircraft industry, when the fate of the nation depended on enough planes to repel enemy bombers. However, unlike the men, the women did not receive full compensation for their injuries, and almost never equal pay for equal work. Indeed, Churchill was so opposed to equality of pay that when women teachers sought parity with men he described the move as "impertinent".

By September 1941, three million women had registered for war work; and in 1943, 90 per cent of single women, and 80 per cent of married women were in some kind of work of national importance; while a year later, they made up no less than 40 per cent of workers in the aircraft industry. Notwithstanding this, when the Minister of Labour raised the age limit of conscription to fifty-one-year-old women, there was an outcry, but he refused to lower it. From then on, any healthy woman who was not working or looking after dependants could be fined or imprisoned for refusing to be directed to employment, wherever it was, and however arduous.

In three short years, the change in women's lives was extraordinary. For the first time, most earned their own money, controlled its expenditure, and were free from the criticism of family and neighbours for so doing. They worked as mechanics, engineers, lorry drivers, fitters, chimney sweeps, railway porters and wheel tappers; they became members of the fire service, crewed barges, unloaded ships' cargos, and repaired gas installations; and though much of the work was dangerous, their horizons broadened beyond their wildest dreams. Then, too, as the war progressed and pay packets increased, women had enough money to enjoy themselves in their few hours off. With their new friends they visited pubs, attended factory and Service dances, and broadened their vocabulary to include not a few swear words. Indeed, everything that the old guard had feared was now happening: the nation's future wives and mothers were being irreparably coarsened, and this despite all the efforts of the government and press to keep them "feminine". However, perhaps the changes accounted for the 32 per cent drop in female suicides.

In September 1939, a magazine reassured its readers that women ambulance drivers "still varnish their nails a rose-pink colour, powder their noses, use lipstick, and make weekly appointments with their hairdresser"; and the cartoonist Gilbert Wilkinson spent the war showing that women in essential work were still empty-headed and frivolous creatures. In 1941, his caption beneath a drawing of a sexy AFS woman on the telephone was: "You know that shop in the High Street where you bought that cute little hat with a veil — well, it's on fire"! Such derogatory captions continued throughout the war, though as women proved their worth, the tone of most did change. For example, in 1941, the caption of an advertisement for the ATS beneath a picture of a *soldier* reads: "No woman will ever have peace in her heart until she helps this man"; while the copy only a few weeks later was changed to: "I am, I think, an intelligent woman. Can you show me that by joining the ATS I shall be given a real chance to use my abilities in full in helping to win this year?" Note the change of appeal from heart to head! But whatever the mixed feelings of the press towards women in the Forces, Civil Defence and industry, it was always wonderfully complimentary to the housewife who, while continuing in her reassuringly traditional role, was burdened beyond belief by the demands of war.

Generally on her own except for dependants, the housewife queued for hours for food and transport, produced meals with less and less, mended and altered a diminishing wardrobe, separated and packaged all waste, grew vegetables, put out incendiary fires in the home, left a key with her neighbour and a bucket of water outside the front door *every* time she went out; and all this on top of sleepless nights of bombing, and the almost impossible task of keeping herself, her dependants and her home clean. As to her work outside, this ranged from air raid warden, ambulance driver, member of a savings group; canteen, rest centre and British restaurant worker; clerk in emergency control centres; pig and chicken keeper; community make-do-and-mend; and organizing the new Citizens Advice Bureau information centres that flourish to this day.

The country had much for which to thank them, and advertisements sang the praise of the housewife over and over again, while boosting their own products by giving advice on how to make the most of ever-diminishing supplies. To give but one infinitely depressing example from 1941: "After washing there is still a teacup full of Lux suds left . . . Empty into a two-pint pudding basin and a pair of silk stockings and two pairs of children's socks are washed through." Helpful though this might have been, I can hear the hollow laughter of bare-legged housewives, for silk stockings were long gone, and I can only assume that the copywriter's girlfriend bought hers on the black market. Still, they say it's the thought that counts, though the action that spoke louder than words was that in the same year a court of appeal ruled that housekeeping savings did not belong to the wife.

Aside from civilian workers, women's greatest contribution to the war effort was in the Auxiliary Territorial Service, the Women's Auxiliary Air Force and the Women's Royal Naval Service; as well as the Nursing and Medical Services, and the Voluntary Aid Detachment where they nursed in such places as the air-raid shelters and in Civil Defence. Because of bomb damage, often they had to crawl under demolished houses in danger of further collapse so as to get to their patients, and many delivered babies in the most bizarre and dangerous surroundings.

In the nursing and medical services, women worked in every theatre of war, and often in the front lines. Many of them were captured, most notably by the Japanese at the fall of Singapore, together with civilian women who had missed or refused evacuation. A shocking sidelight to this was that the British government not only justified our capitulation by stating that the Japanese had far outnumbered our forces, which was a lie; but insinuated that the women who remained and were captured had only themselves to blame, for they had been loath to leave their pampered life. In fact, many of the women remained to help. Midwives, missionaries, and workers in orphanages, to name but a few, had refused to leave their charges to the "tender mercy" of the enemy; while many women doctors and nurses had disobeyed orders to evacuate, so that together with a skeleton staff of locals, they could care for the wounded and dying lying helpless in hospitals.

To add insult to unbelievable injury, those who survived years of horrendous suffering were faced with further humiliation on their release. Because of the rumours that they were spoilt darlings who had refused evacuation, some of the sailors resented the postponement of their demobilization so as to man the ships taking the ex-prisoners home, and their whispered comments must have soured many a journey that should have been heaven. In contrast to the male prisoners who docked in Britain to a tumultuous welcome, the women were brought home in what can only be described as a veil of secrecy. One woman told me that when her ship docked in Liverpool at night, instead of a sea of smiling faces, the quay was empty. The powers-that-be had told the ex-prisoners' families that it was best for their loved ones to be reunited at home! And this was not all, for when the women were issued with train tickets to London, unlike the ship's officers who travelled first class, they had to travel second. "So you see, we went from fourth-class prisoners to second-class citizens." And here we come to the crux of the matter. Like Blacks in the American services, women were regarded as an auxiliary force who worked in safety behind the front lines, for once they were allowed to face the enemy shoulder to shoulder with the men to be wounded and killed beside them, then absolute equality had to be recognized. As it was, many women in *all* the services, myself included, would have wished to be in the front line of the fight for democracy, rather than delegated, at least officially, to the periphery for our own "protection".

Girls who joined the ATS, the WAAF and the WRNS did so from the age of seventeen and in their thousands; and single girls living at home often used the Services as a means of escape, for they could counter their parents' objections with the notion of duty and patriotism. Many a father was caught in the slips by this argument! Once passed as medically fit, they reported to training camps where they lived in Nissen huts and barrack rooms. Their hair was combed for bugs, they were stripped and shoved into ill-fitting uniforms, packed into sleeping quarters that were freezing, square-bashed to exhaustion and route-marched in full kit and gas mask. They were posted to "Ops" rooms, onto gun sites, as wireless operators, ship-to-shore sailors and drivers of convoys. Amazingly, and despite or perhaps because of all this, the majority not only flourished, but discovered a lust for life that was as surprising as it was sudden. There was hardly a NAAFI dance hall and pub that didn't contain their raunchy presence, the anonymity of their uniform even more of a liberation than it was for the men.

In 1941, and for the first time in our history, single women between nineteen and thirty were *conscripted* into the Services, unless they opted to work in the factories; and it could be argued that the women's Services were the first to be democratic, for unlike the men, all had to rise through the ranks.

At seventeen and three-quarters I joined the ATS, and because of my accent was labelled a spoilt middle-class darling by the rest of the barrack room, who had joined up for the twelve shillings and sixpence pay! As far as they were concerned, I would not survive the first week. However, the rigours of army life were as nothing compared to boarding school. After all, I'd had years of community life away from home, timetables and rules, freezing dormitories, rigorous workouts on the playing field, and the hierarchy of monitors, prefects and condescending head girls. No, army life was a doddle, and had the added bonus of no compulsory cold baths, evenings off in the fleshpot of wherever I was stationed, plus the heady freedom of unsupervised leaves rather than school holidays at home. Surprisingly, it was some of the poorer girls who suffered the greatest shock, for they had never been away from their families, and some had never slept in a bed alone. On the first night, the cries of indignation when the corporal insisted on open windows dissolved into such mutterings as "I'll never last the week", "Fresh air's a killer", and numerous threats to go AWOL. For other girls from poor families, army life was an undreamt luxury because of its three meals a day, a change of underclothes, new shoes, and nightwear instead of a vest. Many had never been to the dentist, and their teeth were in such a bad state that our camp dentist told me that sometimes he had to spend an entire session cleaning them, before he could see what needed to be done.

Bearing in mind the narrowness of many women's lives, the mixture of recruits from every strata of society was a revelation. Grouped round a smelly stove in the barrack room, ex-debs, orphans and secretaries swopped their life stories. "Nice" girls learnt the facts of life, never to volunteer, and some fruity language, though surprisingly they were often the first to work out how to get round the system; while it was the sharp Cockney who winkled out what was going on in the camp office, which of the officers were soft, and how to nick from the cookhouse. Most interestingly, by the end of Basic Training, class had all but disappeared and girls had regrouped into victims and survivors. Of course there were always exceptions, and some of the snootier girls retreated behind the *Tatler* and *The Times*, or used their accents to distance themselves from any girl they considered unsuitable. As for our time off, we tended to go to the pub in a gang, our mates giving us the courage to answer back when the soldiers shouted that we were nothing but "officers' groundsheets". And we were called it often, for the ATS was regarded as the Service that took the girls who couldn't get into the WAAF with its pretty blue uniform, or the Wrens who were allowed to wear their own underclothes. Like all those who are seen as the bottom of the heap, we grew more and more aggressive, and many a Wren and WAAF had her hat knocked off while being abused in our very best bad language. Later I was transferred to the FANYs, who were drivers and from whose ranks most of the Intelligence Officers were drawn; for FANYs were allowed to bear arms, and though we were under army discipline, we were termed "of" the army rather than "in" it. It's my theory that this nicety of definition allowed Intelligence to circumvent the government's promise that no Service woman would be sent into enemy territory, let alone be able to receive a VC for bravery. However, many of these girls did see service behind the lines and were wounded or killed, or their health broken for life, but I've yet to see a statue to them, or indeed any of the Services in which over 443,000 women served.

In 1988 it was the fiftieth anniversary of the founding of the ATS, and the fortieth year of its disbanding. I tried hard to interest the television stations in a documentary or drama series on the lines of *Tenko*. No one was interested, and the double anniversary of an army that served its country in peace and in war passed without comment. It was as if we had never existed. Yet an equivalent anniversary of, say, the Fleet Air Arm, would have been celebrated in the press, on radio and in television. Yes Siree!

*

It was not until after the war that women received the vote in France, Italy and Belgium; and Switzerland was neutral in everything except the vote, for women were not given it until 1974.

CHAPTER
EIGHT

Children

Looking back on my childhood in the thirties, is to look back on a time divorced from the reality of an outside world. Nothing impinged on the fastness of the nursery, the junior school and the suitable seaside resort bunged full of other middle-class children. Aside from tradition, we were fashioned by a new breed of paediatricians that insisted on an implacable routine irrespective of the rest of the household, the importance of shoving us into the fresh air whatever the weather, and into hygienic nurseries with safety-barred windows which were unlike any other room in a house. Add to this the influence of cringingly cosy women's magazines featuring such items as curly-headed moppets dressed as fairies and pirates; and mothers and nannies who so prized innocence that children were never allowed to play with anyone "unsuitable", and the result was a life so separate that even our clothes and food were special.

In winter, girls were encased in combinations, or vests with short sleeves; so-called Liberty bodices festooned with buttons; cotton knickers under woollen ones; and the lot topped off by scratchy Fair Isle jerseys over cotton bodices that held up skirts, or smocked woollen dresses that became velvet for high days and holidays. Over these multiple layers we wore wool or tweed coats with stitched Peter Pan collars, hats and gloves. The uniform for summer was a cotton frock, cardigan, sun hat and brown leather sandals in two styles only. Any imaginative deviation was regarded as "common". Boys wore shirts, ties and pullovers, flapping grey flannel shorts that weren't short but reached to the knee, long woollen socks held up by garters, and lace-up shoes. Whatever the design, it was for children only, and there was no such thing as teenage fashion. At a suitable age, boys and girls changed overnight into clothes exactly like their parents.

Except for parties, our food was almost always bland so as not to "heat the blood" and puddings included such colourless and depressing items as rice, tapioca and suet puddings, and a sinister concoction called junket that slid on the spoon and oozed water if left in the dish. All food had to be eaten, or it turned up cold and congealed for the next meal. For teatime there was an extra rule that everything had to be eaten in order: plain bread and butter before bread and jam, biscuits before cakes, and you had to take the nearest one offered on the plate. Innocence, meaning ignorance of the real world, was lovingly preserved by filling our heads with lies: babies were found under gooseberry bushes, or brought by the stork or the doctor in his little black bag; fairies lived under toadstools at the bottom of the garden, and Father Christmas lived in a toy factory at the North Pole. At bedtime, children were read such fantasies as Hans Andersen, *Grimms' Fairy Tales, The Water Babies, The Wind in the Willows, Alice in Wonderland* and *Alice Through the Looking Glass*, some of which were so frightening that most of us had nightmares. Later, there were stories of horses and ponies who suffered and were saved, girl ballet dancers, and male explorers of Dark Continents; plus improbable boarding-school stories in which the hero or heroine was captain of games, captured Bolshevik spies, discovered treasure, and righted wrongs. There was, of course, the wonderful William Brown who was not only grubby but up to no good, and why we were ever allowed to read about him is one of life's mysteries. Still, his influence could always be countered by the endless sayings that governed our behaviour and predicted an unspeakable fate if we didn't toe the line: "If you talk when you eat, you'll swallow your tongue", "If you touch yourself you'll go blind", "If you don't eat your crusts your hair won't curl", "If you make a face when the East Wind blows you'll stay like it", and if you do this or that or the other, the bogey man will get you. We were the victims and the beneficiaries of privilege, who never stopped being told that we were the inheritors of the greatest Empire the world had ever known, and whose father and uncles served in the heart of it, spending their lives civilizing Lesser Breeds in barbaric countries with ghastly climates. Above all, we knew that British children were the luckiest in the world.

What we didn't know was that many of our contemporaries were as undernourished as the "poor little black piccaninnies" in Africa, to whom we sent our pennies; that British slum children suffered and died from infections that could have been cured if their parents had the money to pay for treatment; and that even those children termed "well" were deformed with rickets, infested, and often had no shoes and no change of clothes.

Many of these children lived in housing that was so damp and dilapidated that bugs and dry rot infested the walls, and it was not uncommon for a whole family to live in one room. Children slept two, three or four to a bed, or even under their parents' bed, and when they needed to pee or crap, they did so into a bucket or onto a newspaper. Often water came from a single tap that was shared by the whole house, as was the lavatory, which could be outside at the end of a muddy yard. With such conditions, it's no wonder that infection spread like a fanned flame, and that the small survivors seemed to be from another race with their ringwormed heads, spots, boils, running noses, and dirty faces and clothes. Of course, not all children were like this, but enough not to surprise. And little wonder that we weren't allowed to go near them, though when my friends and I glimpsed them from a bus or car, we were so envious of the way they roamed the streets without an adult — and, what's more, shouting — that we longed to change places; just as they must have longed to change places with us.

Then came the summer of '39 and the government evacuation of children, many of them from the slums, and what had been ignored was scattered throughout the country for all to see and abhor.

The evacuation began on 30 August, and was organized by the Ministry of Health and Transport, and the Board of Education. After weeks of heart-searching, during which parents balanced the dangers of bombing against sending their children to an unknown destination to be looked after by strangers, those courageous enough to opt for their offspring's safety woke them at dawn, dressed and washed them for what might be the last time, and took them to an assembly point. To ease the separation, many told their children that they were going on holiday, and some even carried buckets and spades. At the moment of parting, mothers handed their children a case or paper bag containing spare clothes if they had them, a toothbrush, comb, handkerchief and enough food for the day, before fastening a label on their coats with the child's name and home address. Then they waved them goodbye. Which was the most painful I don't know: the ones who cried, or the many who clambered happily into the requisitioned buses, or sang as they walked behind their teachers carrying banners to identify their group.

In a few days, a million and a half of the nation's children left the cities, most of them by train. They poured into stations until it seemed that the forecourts had been invaded by a Lilliputian race; while above their heads, teachers and volunteers tried to keep order by shouting instructions, though even their authoritative voices could not top the chatter, laughter, shrieks and screams that emitted from mouths already smudged with dirt, let alone the loudspeakers begging someone to collect little so-and-so from the station master's office. Amongst this multitude, as well as the blind, the crippled, the retarded and a legion of wheelchairs, mothers struggled to carry their babies, their offspring's heads bobbing about like buoys in a storm.

Once on the train, children battled for the window-seats or those next to the corridor, the more adventurous swinging from the luggage racks or climbing into them, and almost immediately there were demands for the lavatory. From then on until the children arrived at "destinations unknown", the two-way traffic in the corridors was constant, the wilder ones shouting to friends and enemies along the route, and even managing a passing fisticuffs.

Luckily for the adults, once the journey was underway,

their charges began to settle. It was late summer and hot, they'd risen at dawn, and cried their goodbyes or sensed their parents misery, and those that didn't doze stared out at a countryside that was often as strange as it was bewildering. Before television, many children had never seen a field, a cow or any other livestock, let alone a vast space without houses. Mile after mile they travelled through an alien landscape, many suffering from travel sickness or the first pangs of homesickness, and a few were trapped on a train for as long as twelve hours. Worse still, many trains had no corridors, and the adults had to deal with the children's needs as best they could. Given the hot weather and cramped space, the conditions must have been indescribable, let alone the smell.

At last, and very often at long last, the evacuees arrived at their destination. Most were exhausted, thirsty, hungry and bewildered; they had no idea where they were, or if they'd ever see their families and homes again. I witnessed a party of these children arriving at Swindon: lines of crumpled figures clutching luggage that might be heavy but at least was familiar, and with that absorbed and stoical expression so typical of all refugees. Ahead of them lay a bus journey, perhaps hours in a village hall being inspected by locals who might or might not take them in, to be followed by yet another journey with a stranger who spoke in a strange accent, and took them to a strange house where they ate strange food, before falling into a strange and lonely bed. Many were separated from their brothers and sisters, and many more from their friends; for while the theory was to keep families and, if possible, school groups together, in practice it was any port in a storm. Indeed, though the assembly and transportation had been made in some detail, it was the women's voluntary Services that picked up the pieces at the destinations, and had to cope with those who were lost, who couldn't be placed and had to be housed and fed, sometimes for days; plus the many other loose ends that even the most imaginative had never envisaged. For all that, it was a magnificent operation, for in the minimum of time, the nation's children, mothers and babies *were* sent to a place of safety, and may owe their lives to the vast army of people who made it possible.

Once settled, most of the children adapted to country life and grew to love it, though initially there was much animosity between the evacuees and the local children, especially at school. In the village where I was evacuated, confrontations took place in the main street, evacuees and locals eyeing each other suspiciously as they hurled insults and stones; and at snowball time the battles were ferocious, each side considering the other to be an enemy far more deadly than any Nazi. In the end, the fights became a ritual and were much enjoyed, and woe betide any adult who tried to stop them, for all would unite against a common and far more powerful foe. Indeed, as the months went by, country food and air, the fields, woods and rivers in which to run and swim, wrought such a change that pale faces filled out and grew rosy, muscles bulged where there had been none before, and many grew as much as an inch in two months.

For the few, lives were made miserable by sadistic adults, or those so greedy that they had only taken them in because of the boarding allowance. Some of these children were used as free labour around the house and on the land, their desperate letters home destroyed by the monsters who were meant to be taking care of them.

As the months passed and the expected air raids failed to materialize, many evacuees returned home, though some were re-evacuated because of the Blitz and again when the rockets began. Indeed, the government was so concerned about the return of so many that the Minister of Health issued the following statement: "This war has forced terribly hard decisions on mothers in towns . . . Many, far too many alas, have since brought their children back. Some of these children have drifted back to death. Others are maimed for life."

Of the children who remained in the country, many grew to love their adopted parents, and sometimes more than their natural ones; but then travel was difficult and sometimes too expensive, so that the space between visits could become longer and longer or even peter out altogether. For some parents, it was the visits themselves that were too painful to face. Imagine your children turning into strangers with odd accents and chattering about unknown people and places; and when they asked about home, how could you tell them that it had been demolished and that this or that relative and friend had been killed? No. Better to change the subject and not have much to say. Nevertheless, many parents did visit regularly, and when the war ended the majority of children were happy to return home, though a few were broken-hearted, and some remained with their adopted parents because they'd been orphaned or deserted. For instance, often the father had been killed and the mother had made a new life for herself free from commitments; or, in the casual way of war, had just drifted. But whatever happened to these children, most of them were in far better health than when they left the cities, especially if they'd lived in the slums, and all carried a knowledge of other communities and ways of life that would stay with them for ever.

For the city children who remained with their parents, or more usually with their mothers, life was lived at its extremes. There was the terror of the bombing, the fear or actual loss of relatives and friends, homes, and much-loved toys; and the never-ending broken or sleepless nights. However, this was more than balanced by the bonuses. Not that adults saw it in this light. Most mothers worked full- or part-time, so that their children were able to run free and have splendid adventures on the bomb sites and in half-demolished houses. Imagine the joy of your very own den where a swing could be hung from the rafters, and with real stairs to defend when a rival gang came to capture your forces. Think of the dressing-up clothes, when you could rifle through abandoned trunks and wardrobes, and swank about in grown-up jackets and evening dresses and costume jewellery. As for school, with some partly demolished and so many air raids, timetables went to the wall, and it was not uncommon to attend only for the morning or afternoon. For the rest of the time, many helped the war effort, and this gave them a unique sense of importance, plus the added kick of being able to bully grown-ups. They collected every kind of scrap; looked after pigs and chickens and rabbits; acted as messengers; and took part in the Savings Weeks, where they'd be part of a patriotic tableau wearing fancy dress and stamping about pretending to be soldiers and nurses. Sometimes children organized their own charity entertainments which before the war might only have been tolerated, but now were encouraged; as was digging up the garden to grow vegetables and the chance to find buried treasure. But best of all was the invasion scare, when children had a field day devising booby traps to hinder the enemy, for if anyone had perfected the art of hindrance, it was those with years of experience playing cops and robbers. And throughout it all, and perhaps best of all, was the new and easy intimacy with parents. There was something about a darkened shelter, of sitting close together as the bombs rained down, that bridged any gap of experience and years. What more natural, when a mother might be killed, for her to share her hopes and pass on her memories: this is how it was, and this, and this, and don't you ever forget it. And if the next day she discounted the confidences, most children knew why, for fear is understood by everyone, however young.

One of the many tragedies of the air raids was that families dispersed and where once there had been grandparents, aunts, uncles and cousins, often only a mother was left. Then she, too, might be forced to move, so that children lost their few remaining friends and had to make new ones, and at a new school with a new curriculum. Bad enough to be surrounded by strangers, without dropping from fourth to fifteenth in the class, because history and geography lessons were no longer about the Elizabethans and the effects of the Ice Age. This happened to me, though I was already bottom of the class and could sink no further. I'd been studying the Middle Ages, whereas my new school was well into the Napoleonic Wars. Ever since, whatever happened between 1300 and the end of the eighteenth century has been hazy to say the least.

The loss of so many baby-minding relatives was a terrible blow to mothers who wanted to work and had young children, for either they were forced to stay at home or leave them with minders who might or might not be reliable. Luckily the government needed the mothers as much as they needed or wanted to work, and though it took some time to set up nursery schools, by the end of 1943, 65,000 children were attending 1,450 nurseries, which puts to shame the few nurseries that struggle to survive now.

Most of these wartime nurseries were wonderfully run, putting into practice all the idealism of a country fighting for a better life. The staff was headed by trained personnel, and the majority of the nurseries were airy, full of light and served balanced meals topped up by free milk and orange or rosehip syrup. On arrival, a child had its own peg on which to hang outdoor clothes, before putting on a pinafore for a morning of games, singing and simple lessons, followed by lunch, a rest indoors or in the garden if the weather was fine, more play and then tea. Every nursery aimed to teach the children to feed themselves with reasonable table manners, to clear away, to dress, tie shoe laces, wash, clean their teeth, and go to the lavatory unaided. And because factories and many offices worked long shifts, a mother could bring her child before breakfast, and collect it in the evening after supper. Not only did this save her hours of queuing for food, but it gave her just enough time to tidy the home. If the child was very young, it was lifted out of the cot still asleep, and taken to the nursery to continue sleeping. Used to community living from a young age, these children learnt to give and take and to help new arrivals, the perfect training for the struggles and privations in which they would grow up after the war.

Some of the nurseries were in the country and residential, so as to help children recover from the air raids, or to give exhausted mothers a rest. One such nursery took in many badly blitzed and stunned children, and set great store by the right diet to aid recovery and good health. Here is a typical menu: Breakfast — rolled oats and milk, with grated carrot and beetroot, wholemeal bread with jam or honey; Lunch: meat or fish most days, plus salad of grated turnip, carrot, beetroot, lettuce, chopped onions and herbs, bread with cheese sauce to give extra protein, and raw or stewed fruit. No drink was allowed with this meal; Tea: salad of lettuce, tomato, carrots and radishes, wholemeal bread with jam, and milk. All refined and packet food was banned!

Another terrible tragedy of the war was the thousands of children who became orphans, some having witnessed their parents' death, or been trapped beside their corpses as they stiffened and grew cold. On 2 August 1941, amongst the many children admitted to Dr Barnardo's, was a baby boy. Nobody knew his exact age, only that he was about thirteen months, and had been rescued from a dug-out, bruised and suffering from shock. Often it took months and sometimes years before these children ceased wetting the bed, suffering from nightmares, sudden terrors during the day, and the nervous rages that tried to express what they couldn't voice. Once recovered sufficiently, even they were encouraged to help the war effort, each orphanage adopting its own minesweeper or some other unit, the older children knitting scarves and writing letters to the men and women, and together with the smallest, collecting money for their very own cause.

To me there is something incredibly moving in the efforts of even the youngest to contribute to the common cause, and in so doing, to share so much; and how heartbreaking to look round now and see how little is shared and how many are isolated. Cut off from the weather by central heating and air conditioning, millions travel in cars where everyday sounds are muffled by radios or cassettes, and spend the end of the day in yet another perfectly constructed unit of self-sufficiency called home.

At least during the war children understood how others lived, though many were forced into the tougher world of work as young as fourteen. In 1941, a survey showed that nearly half the boys and girls between fourteen and eighteen worked at least nine hours a day, plus overtime. Also, because of the blackout and the low wattage of bulbs, many suffered from eyestrain; while in winter they were forced to spend their days in overcoats and mittens. At my own school, there was always a long line of chilblain sufferers queuing for treatment, but we still counted ourselves lucky compared with those who had been packed off abroad.

At the beginning of the war, many children were sent to the United States, which in 1940 passed a bill to amend their Neutrality Act so that ships could carry evacuees to safety. However, the greatest danger was the journey, and after a ship full of children was sunk by the enemy, the exodus all but stopped. I might have been on that ship, for my mother was planning to send me to relatives in Pittsburgh, and I'll never forget my despair when the lights went up in a cinema, and I remembered that soon I would be leaving all that I loved. Despite the bombing and privations, the idea was so terrible that I begged her to let me stay. I wasn't the only one, for some of my friends were in the same position, and we actually discussed running away rather than being forced to desert. And if "desert" sounds too strong a word, that is what we felt. But then, I am convinced that adults did not give children credit for a broader loyalty beyond their family, let alone any understanding of what would have happened if the country had been defeated.

Even before the war, there had been stories of what was happening to children under the Nazis. As early as the mid-thirties, we'd met Jewish children who had fled from Hitler, and who told us how they'd been persecuted at school, how their dolls with blonde hair had been snatched away because a Jew mustn't play with Aryan toys, and even how they'd been spat on and kicked. Then, during the war, we'd heard whispers of how blond children in occupied countries were being taken from their parents and "given" to German families; how crippled children had disappeared; and even that thousands of children were being tortured and murdered. Not that we confided our fears to adults, who would have told us that we were imagining things, and that nobody was ever cruel to children. We knew better.

CHAPTER
NINE

The Old

At the outbreak of war, the old could look back on a youth where the certainties of class and the structure of authority seemed absolute; and if God was not an Englishman, then He was certainly on their side. Despite the intervening years of upheaval — five monarchs, the Boer and First World Wars, votes for women, the General Strike and the Depression — in many ways the old remained Victorians. With few exceptions, they were God-fearing, respectful of authority, and above all set the greatest store by their independence, especially if they were poor.

Before Social Security, public charity was so degrading that many chose suicide rather than accept it, especially the humiliation of the workhouse. Hardly changed since Dickens's day, they were terrible places, where the old slept in dormitories of forty or more beds, and lived by a bleak and strict timetable that would not have shamed a penal colony. Sexes were separated, and married couples were only allowed to meet at a time set by the authorities. With such a future for those who became destitute, it's no wonder that people clung to poorly paid jobs and bad conditions if a pension was guaranteed; while others would go without necessities so as to contribute to the National Insurance.

Despite this, in 1936 only half of the over-sixty-fives who had contributed to the scheme were eligible for a pension of ten shillings a week, plus as much again for a dependent wife; and this at a time when ten shillings was below the official poverty line. For the rest who had failed to keep up their payments, or who had no means of support, either their families were forced to care for them, or, as a last resort, they could apply for Poor Relief and the withering humiliation of a Means Test. Imagine having to face a row of officials who cross-questioned you on every possession you had, even the most personal, and who demanded financial details of all near relations from whom they might claw back any money they handed over. And if by luck or the selling of furniture and treasures, you somehow managed to scrape by until seventy, then you could apply for the Lloyd George pension, though even this depended on a Means Test.

However the poor managed to obtain their pittance, their retirement was eked out in penury, and it says much for the store they set by respectability that most managed to put something by for their funeral, though even the simplest cost as much as £13–£15, plus the cost of "decent black" for the surviving spouse, and a "little something" to offer the mourners afterwards. This final ritual was considered so important that some literally starved themselves to death so that they might be "seen off in a proper manner", rather than being buried on the Parish.

Of course, there were what was still called the Undeserving Poor, who didn't give a damn about appearances, but they were rare, for the mass of the older and poorer population prided themselves on "doing the right thing". Despite rheumatism and arthritis, the women scrubbed their doorsteps, starched the lace curtains that hid the scrimping within, and together with their husbands that had survived, attended church and praised the Lord for the magnificence of His bounty. On Armistice Day, the men polished their medals of possibly two wars, and when the guns fired the salute on the eleventh hour of the eleventh day of the eleventh month, their backs straightened as they stood to honour the dead and the country that bore them.

At the outbreak of war, pensioners tended to stay put, even if they lived in the cities. Here's the old woman in our typical surburban street, who's living on thirteen shillings and sixpence a week. Luckily she owns the house, though with no furniture upstairs because she's sold it, she daren't let the rooms in case the neighbours find out. Besides, the roof leaks and there's mildew on the ceiling, so she lives on the ground floor in the front room. She buys her food from the grocer's and butcher's vans that visit the street, and they pretend to believe she has a dog for whom she buys bones and the discarded outer leaves of vegetables. These she boils into soup on the open fire so as to save lighting the stove. Once a month the fishmonger calls, and he sells her fish heads for a cat that never appears. It is very quiet in the house, for she can't afford a radio, so she talks to the photograph of her parents. Once a week she puts sixpence into her funeral fund, and somehow she's managed to save almost £28. "I'll go to my Maker in style," she tells her Mama and Papa. "Two black horses and cut-glass windows in the hearse, and my coffin'll have solid brass handles, and with no relations I'll not have the cost of a car, so I can afford a nice solid headstone." She doesn't understand about the inflation, so she goes to bed with a happy heart.

At the beginning of the war, the lives of the old changed very little, but as it continued and the manpower shortage increased, they were wooed back to work. Women helped out in the shelters and air-raid posts, their expertise at sewing much in demand by the WVS and clothing depots; and their talent for making dishes out of next to nothing often became the star turn in the British restaurants and canteens for the homeless. For the many old soldiers, there was the glory of once more bearing arms in the Home Guard; and for the rest who were able-bodied there were so many part- and full-time jobs that for the first time in their lives they were able to pick and choose. Of course, the old suffered terribly in the air raids, especially if they lost their homes and had to be moved to makeshift quarters; and more than any other group, they suffered from the lack of fuel, dying in their thousands during the freezing winters of '40 and '47. But again, and like our old woman in the suburban street, at least they were needed once more, and were no longer cut off and listening to the tick of a clock marking the minutes to their death.

Teachers in particular were wooed back into the workforce, including one of the two real-life teachers on whom James Hilton based his famous character Mr Chips. Luckily for the old-timers, teaching methods did not change from year to year as they do now, and at least the map of the world had remained the same for twenty years!

For those who survived to take part in the victory celebrations, many must have viewed the future with a mixture of hope and despair. Here are some of them, sitting at the table in paper hats and eating the Victory tea in our suburban street. Here's Harry, who grew such wonderful cabbages and tomatoes, and had such a way with Elsie the pig; and Tom who worked in the air-raid post brewing up and keeping the place ship-shape; and old Barnaby who never stopped grumbling until his house was hit, when he became the life and soul of No. 20, who'd dreaded his arrival and now adore him. And there's Elsie, and Rose and Heather, who did such sterling work at the Resettlement Centre and Make-do-and-mend, and could always be relied on to babysit far into the night. They all look happy enough now, exchanging memories of the air raid when Mr Saunders ran into the street minus his trousers and wearing odd socks; and what about old Barnaby who's been allocated a spanking new pre-fab house, and has started to gripe again? But sometimes, when nobody is looking, their eyes grow bleak. Will life drift back to "good morning" and "good evening" and not a word in between? And will the toddlers stop calling them Auntie and Uncle once they're big enough to go to school? And what of the day when they'll be too old to look after themselves and have to go into a Home? Not that it'll be the workhouse, mark you, for something better is promised, and about time too. But will they look back on the war as a golden time, and bore all the inmates silly with the memory of this celebration today? I think they might.

CHAPTER
TEN

Fashion

Clothes reflect our feelings and the attitude of the society in which we live, so that to look through the British fashion plates of the inter-war years is to glean something of those times: the "short back and sides" hairstyle of the men following the First World War; the wide Oxford bags of the thirties that reflected the revolt of university youth against the ethos of their parents; the casual flannel trousers and jackets that hinted at a slackening of formality.

For women, above all, fashion demonstrated their degree of freedom or restriction: the loose bodice, short skirt and bare arms of the liberated Flapper girl of the twenties, evolving into the curves of bias cutting and a longer skirt as unemployment rose and women were celebrated as wives and mothers who stayed at home. Their hair reflected this even more starkly, for the easy-to-manage and straight Eton crop of the Flapper gave way to styles that were longer and curly, and were described by that most telling of words: soft. Indeed, by 1939 curls were mandatory, and advertising campaigns hastened to rescue the millions of women suffering from straight hair. "Nestol makes baby's hair curly", "Glorious curls — lasting and natural with Lorelox", "The only way to natural curls is Vosemar". Blonde ringlet-infested moppets and permed adults smiled out from every women's magazine and newspaper, for fair hair was almost as essential, reflecting as it did the perfect Aryan and the heroines of the cinema: Shirley Temple, Jean Harlow and the enchanting Jean Arthur. To show off their hair to the best advantage, stars were often photographed as wind-blown outdoor girls, though in reality their heads would be covered by a hat, for it was *the* symbol of ladylike refinement that reached back to the Judean Christian insistence that females must cover their heads. Indeed, such was the pre-war mania for hats that some kept them on in the house, and that most respectable of women, the cleaner, wore hers as if it was a badge of office: severe enough to demonstrate reliability, and hard enough to show that she'd stand no nonsense.

Gloves were yet another necessity, and in "polite society" it was frowned on to be seen putting them on out of doors, for all well-brought-up women should be perfectly groomed before leaving the house. Even as late as the mid-forties when a man gave me a lift to my grandmother's, her greatest shock was not that I'd placed myself in the compromising position of being in an enclosed space unchaperoned, but that I was wanton enough not to wear gloves.

However, for the rest of the nation the war justified many compromises, and the shabbier you appeared, the greater your patriotism. The first innovation was the siren suit, which within months changed from a sensible covering to high fashion. It even grew wide shoulders, for as men donned uniforms so civilian clothes reflected the military line. Besides, as women shouldered more and more responsibility, so this could be demonstrated literally, together with larger pockets for identity cards and ration books, shoulder bags to leave hands free for carrying endless comforts to the shelter, and hoods to protect the head. And the hat? Older women clung to it as the last vestige of a crumbling civilization; while the younger generation abandoned it except for special occasions, for not only had the Archbishop of Canterbury given women dispensation to be hatless in church, but they required precious clothing coupons which could be better spent on necessities.

To balance this austerity, women's hairstyles became more and more complicated, and bore such patriotic names as "The Victory V" and "Montgomery's Sweet", and were much favoured in the Services, where a hairstyle was the only way left to express individuality. However, wondrous styles demand longish hair, and this was anathema to sergeants, for the rule was that every single hair must be well clear of the collar. If even one wisp touched cloth, the sergeant would close in from the rear, and with mouth pressed to the offender's ear, bellow: "I am *standing* on your hair!" But women can be stubborn, and while some cut it, many twisted and curled the lot on to the top of their heads, anchoring the weight with enough clips to conduct lightning, and whose sound as they cascaded down during the silence of Church Parade was as the tinkling of tiny bells. Far more practical was the use of the sanitary towel, whose end-loops were linked by a length of elastic or tape, the resulting circle placed on the head with the towel at the back, so that the hair could be tucked round it in a neat roll. The beauty of this innovation was that when a period started protection was to hand, the lot being whipped off and used elsewhere!

In the factories, where safety regulations forced girls to cover their hair with a triangular scarf tied in the style of a Black Mammy, many pulled a hank of hair forward and rolled it into a fringe anchored with clips. Tragically, the "cascading" had a far more dire result than in the Services, for as the fringe fell forward into the machinery, some were literally scalped. Despite its macabre associations, the Black Mammy style was taken up by many civilian women who had replaced a hat with a scarf, and which, because it was longer, was twisted into a turban. In no time, the fashion houses had taken this up, and turbans were seen everywhere and in every kind of fabric.

It wasn't until the 1 June 1941 that clothes rationing was introduced in the form of clothing coupons, the number for any particular item depending on how much cloth and labour had been used. Thus overcoats required the most, with dresses, shirts, cardigans and underclothes scaled down accordingly. At this time, only women's clothes changed according to fashion, for men's clothes had hardly altered for years, so that as long as a male civilian had *something* to wear, their wives and daughters regarded their coupons as a bank on which they could draw when their own were spent. Only when a man's clothes were literally falling apart could he be sure that the piracy would cease, and even the coupons of the dead had a way of vanishing before they were cold.

As the years passed, clothing coupons suffered the same fate as food points and had to last for longer periods, or were increased for each article, the Board of Trade extending its territory to include household linen, upholstery and curtain material. Finally, the only materials left with which to create a new outfit were sugar bags, sacking, hessian, scrim and canvas. However, need is a splendid spur, and innovation replaced what the authorities had taken away. Jerseys were unravelled and reknitted, larger clothes cut down to make smaller ones, onion water and herbs brewed to dye faded cloth until, like the food recipes, clothing could be made of the strangest ingredients. For instance, a curtain that had been replaced by blackout material could be made into a skirt and decorated with horizontal stripes made from part of a counterpane; the rest of it being turned into cushion covers, jacket linings, and a women's jerkin bound with chamois leather that had been purchased at the beginning of the war for cleaning windows. Even the fur of the rabbit bred for the cooking pot was put to good use, and was made into gloves, collars, muffs and various linings. Indeed, the odder the original source, the more we boasted, and "Guess what this was?" became a regular part of our conversation.

At seventeen and a half, I became almost suicidal in my quest for a grown-up hat, for an elderly man of thirty-six had asked me out on my very first "date". By dint of cutting up the brown velvet jacket of a woman who'd died, I made a very fair copy of the pill-box worn by Alice in Wonderland, to which I added a fetching valance at the rear. Unfortunately, I'd glued the velvet to cardboard, and it was very hot in the restaurant, so that by the time we'd reached the entrée a strange fishy smell was rising from my head, tunnels of goo trickling down my forehead and into my hair. Sadly, the man of the world was not as sophisticated as I'd imagined, and I was hustled out of the restaurant before I'd managed to gulp down the pudding.

In 1942, the Board of Trade introduced restrictions on the design of clothes so as to save on labour and material. Men's jackets had to be single-breasted, with not more than three pockets and buttons down the front, while no buttons were allowed on the cuffs. Trouser waistbands lost their elastic, and the width of trouser legs was restricted to nineteen inches at the most, and with no turn-ups. For some reason this was seen as a terrible blow to men's dignity, and some purchased trousers that were too long so that they could turn up the bottoms. However, boys suffered a far greater indignity, for they were not allowed out of shorts until at least eleven or twelve, and as this was seen as one of the milestones of growing up, indignation knew no bounds. For women, jackets had the same restrictions as the men's plus restricted pleating in the skirts which could only be a certain length. However, it was the girls who left school who suffered the greatest humiliation, for they received no extra coupons, and were forced to continue wearing parts of their uniform. I was one of this number, and had to suffer the humiliation of exposing my school underclothes at the Army Medical, and then having to report to camp in what was obviously a school coat. It was around that time that I developed a loathing for any woman who had left school before the war, because most of them had a cherished pair of high-heeled shoes, whereas my lace-ups were replaced by ones with a miserable two-inch heel, plus a pair with hinged wooden soles to save leather, and which squeaked when I walked. Worse was to come! After telling my mother that I was to be posted overseas, she gave away all the civilian clothes I'd managed to beg or borrow, so that when I was discharged instead, it was the shame of the school uniform all over again. As one of my flatmates remarked so inaccurately: "You're all fur coat and no knickers", for I had spent my demob coupons on outer finery, and was forced to put on and remove the dreaded khaki bloomers in the fastness of the bathroom where no one could see me. Not that I didn't have the odd triumph: the acquired scrim that was used to line coffins, and which was turned into an evening skirt; an opera cloak that was pilfered from a dressing-up box despite the screams of its six-year-old owner; and a length of spanking new white nylon that was used to make parachutes, which I made into a blouse. This was not entirely successful, for parachute nylon was so stiff that the darts stuck out in points, and my breasts appeared to have the shape and consistency of a pair of steel cones. Still, most of us looked odd in one way or another, if only that our dressing gowns were made from old blankets, and our legs ran gravy browning whenever we were caught in the rain.

The lack of a fashionable wardrobe did not end with the war. Far from it, for rationing continued until 1949, and many were driven to augment their clothes in the Services' Surplus Stores, buying such items as oiled naval jerseys, RAF shirts, duffle coats and the prized British Warm. This was a three-quarter-length coat made for army officers, and quite a few men elevated their old army rank by pretending it had been theirs during the war. In the end, it endowed the wearers with a shady past whether they merited it or not, and Uncle Bobby, who was still on the lookout for any man who dared to make eyes at my sainted aunt, insisted that the tell-tale signs of a Rotter was a British Warm, a scarf tucked in at the neck and brown suede shoes, or indeed any with crepe rubber soles.

In some ways, the immediate post-war clothes predated the Unisex Look, for women, too, wore duffle coats, the oiled jersey and cut-down Servicemen's shirts with added darts. And a sorry lot we looked, for the duffle coat was invariably too big, and what with the sleeves hanging over our hands, and the hem somewhere mid-calf, it appeared as if our heads were poking up out of woolly tents.

Then, suddenly, Paris launched the New Look and we gasped. Gone were the military shoulders, the short hemlines and the restrictions on buttons, pockets and pleats. In their places were creations that were so feminine that they looked almost Victorian, with small sloping shoulders, tight armholes, tiny waists that could only be achieved with a "Waspy" corset, enough material in the ankle-length skirts to double as a marquee, and delicate tottery shoes. And it wasn't just the shape that bewitched us, but an avalanche of decorations: sequins, beads, embroidery, lace and as many buttons as the designer saw fit to scatter. In truth, the New Look was sheer heaven and unmitigated hell, for who could afford the coupons to replace a whole wardrobe, when anything less would have looked ridiculous. In the end, it was back to cutting up old curtains yet again. A skirt was lengthened by inserting contrasting material, and which, if it was part of a suit, had the same material added to collar and cuffs. We nipped in waists, ripped out shoulder-pads and re-inserted sleeves, and if we were very nimble-fingered, we fashioned a *hat*, for fashionable heads were once again covered. I managed to go one better, for mine was a straw boater that Uncle Jack had worn some forty years earlier, and which, by dint of swathing the crown with a strip of lace curtain dyed to match my outfit, made me look as old-fashioned as the new fashion demanded.

What none of my friends or myself realized was that our appearance now mirrored the role allotted to us by the Powers-that-be: women who looked like "real" women, and who with any luck might behave like them, happily returning to the role of wife and mother, and leaving the jobs to the men who were being demobbed. However, what we *did* realize, especially if we continued working, was that we'd lost the freedom of wartime fashion, for hats blew off in the wind, armholes were so skimped that we were unable to lift our arms above shoulder level, waists were so tight that we developed indigestion and were out of breath if we ran, and skirts were so long and voluminous that getting on a bus was a nightmare.

In truth, once again we had been well and truly hobbled.

CHAPTER
ELEVEN

Save!

Since the Industrial Revolution, Britain had had to import most of her raw materials: items as varied as cotton from India, rubber from Malaya, timber from Norway, silk from China, and scrap metal from the United States. Then, with the enemy occupation of Western Europe and the blockade at sea, raw materials became so scarce that the nation was forced to set to and save, and with a fanatical zeal which could well serve as an example today.

Anticipating our loss of raw materials even before the heavy losses at sea, the Limitation of Supplies Order halted the manufacture of luxury goods, as well as cutting back on much else so as to concentrate supplies on war production. Such so-called fripperies as gardening tools, bath plugs, pencils, ball cocks and even sewing machines disappeared from the shops; though why the Civil Service included paper clips is very odd, when they must have been as essential to the running of their departments as the ubiquitous tea-break. Of the items that were cut back, a few were offered first to those in most need: thermos flasks to Civil Defence, clocks to shift workers, and musical instruments to the BBC, and if the latter isn't proof of attention to detail, I don't know what is!

The result of this efficiency was that within a year such

items as glasses, kettles, perambulators, toys, furniture and cosmetics became in such short supply that the nation learnt to make do with the most unlikely substitutes: boot-black was brushed on to eyelashes, red dye mixed with cream rubbed into cheeks, buttons became earrings, and jam jars were carted to parties and pubs as substitute glasses. Even second-hand shops that before the war had been used only by the poorest were now frequented by Doxies and Duchesses alike, in a desperate bid to find curtains thick enough for the blackout; while the second-hand furniture shops did such a brisk trade that a fresh stock was sold before it was unloaded.

By the spring of 1941, nearly a million and a half had become homeless in London alone, and such was the demand for furniture and bedding that the Board of Trade devised a unit allowance to cover basic needs, all else having to be scrounged or made out of what was to hand. Wooden fruit boxes were turned into shelves and bookcases, non-coupon hessian and flour sacks became curtains and covers, and bottles stood in for table lampstands. As for wall decoration, by 1942 the cream, green and brown paint so beloved by government departments was all that was available, and with wallpaper long gone, rooms were distempered. Indeed, such was the boring uniformity that the houseproud were driven to painting their own murals so as to add some colour, and a friend of mine who was a Free French officer with a talent for drawing, spent all his spare time embellishing restaurant walls in return for free meals.

By the autumn of that year, new austerity regulations had extended conformity to packaging, and all decoration was banned; while such non-essentials as soup spoons disappeared for the duration. Even the lowly teaspoon was so difficult to replace that restaurants and canteens tied a single spoon to the till by a piece of string. Not that this was foolproof against the ruthless customer, for in the gloom of the blackout it was easy enough to cut the string and pocket the prize. As one of my light-fingered army mates boasted: "I've managed to nick a whole dozen for my bottom drawer!" But then, she was the proud possessor of four whole yards of elastic, which was one of the most maddening of all the shortages. Indeed, as elastic slackened and perished in the nation's knickers, many gave them up altogether rather than suffer the bumps of knot added to knot, or the pain of tape that had to be tied so tightly in order to do the job that weals developed around the waist.

It was in 1942 that the dearth of essentials became so pressing that the government introduced the Utility Label for goods that used the minimum of material in a strictly limited and controlled range; though given these strictures, most were so well designed that the furniture is still in use today. As more and more goods disappeared from the shops, the utility range expanded to include such diverse items as torches, clothes, lamps, blankets and perambulators; and though they all gave good service, their uniformity was as depressing as their austerity.

As we learnt to make do, so we were exhorted to save; radio, posters, newspapers and magazines telling us not only how to, but what to save, with the Ministry of Works giving details of scrap metal collection, while the Ministry of Supply masterminded all else. In the end, the remorseless propaganda was so successful that it became a point of pride to give more than the neighbours, and the real fanatic donated personal treasures that could never be replaced.

Indeed, housewives were so eager to prove that they, too, could contribute to the war effort, that photographs of loved ones were prized from antique metal frames, cut-steel buckles unpicked from belts, and pipe cleaners substituted for the irreplaceable metal hair-curlers. Even the children were cajoled to give their tin soldiers and train sets, though with the literalism of the young, they managed to take their revenge. "But Mum, pipe cleaners have metal insides, so why don't you give them as well? And why aren't the police giving up their handcuffs, and what about your corsets? I mean, Jim's Mum has pulled out all her metal bits and she's even fatter!"

However, it was in the kitchen that the greatest sacrifices were made. Cooks have strong feelings about their utensils: the wedding-present saucepan; the poacher used by Granny; the kettle in which an exact teapotful can be gauged by the sound of the water filling it; and yet they gave them all, and, what's more, willingly. I am ashamed to say that my aunt's patriotism, which had been so exemplary during the jam-making, did not come up to scratch when it came to the specially designed saucepans for the Aga cooker. Motor mechanic Aunt Pam made her excuses from under a car she was servicing for the vicar: "Ratio of heat lost to metal gained, ain't worth the candle!" While Aunt Grace, who didn't give a damn about science, bemoaned the loss of objects that were aesthetically acceptable even to her stringent standards. Uncle Charles would have none of it. Wrenching the pans from my aunt's grasp, he drilled holes in the bottoms before slinging the lot onto the scrapheap. "I'll not have some Quisling flogging the stuff to some rotten black marketeer," he explained in his best army bellow, and from then on most of the meals were burnt.

One hilarious outcome of emptying the nation's kitchens was the sight of wild-eyed women glaring up at a flypast of planes. "There goes my mangle" one would exclaim, to be topped by another shaking her fists at the sky and screaming that her "whole bloody kitchen had taken wing".

Together with scrap metal, everything saved had to be separated, and front gardens and pavements became crammed with bins and sacks for paper, rubber, tin, bones, rags, cardboard, bottles, jars, and scraps for the pigs. Nor could they be slung in anyhow: tins had to be flattened, bones cleaned and dried, while certain items had to be taken back to the shops, who would then return them to the manufacturers. For instance, toothpaste tubes, which contained both tin and lead, had to be returned to the chemist who, in government parlance, was an "Authorized Collector"!

To make sure that the nation was kept up to snuff, campaigns were launched featuring one specific item which, in the case of the jam jar, was collected by children. The unlooked for power that this gave them was so heady that occasionally they went beyond the call of duty and terrorized whole neighbourhoods. Packs of Brownies and Cubs would storm the sanctuary of a father's shed, or spoon out the last of a precious dollop of jam, so as to add just one jar to the cart that was pulled by the heftiest child in the pack; and the sight of a phalanx of uniformed tots must have signalled the slamming of many a door before the store cupboard was sniffed out and ransacked. Such was their ruthless efficiency that the money collected from the sale of jars paid for an aircraft and lifeboat. How the Brown Owls must have cheered!

However, it was the scrapmetal drive that topped all

records, and to give but one example: in April 1940, when 10,000 food tins made up a ton worth £1 15*s*., £1,250,000 was netted. Little wonder, then, that the Public Works Department became so obsessive that they were indifferent to the treasures that were melted down. All right, so it was necessary to pull up the railings of houses and public spaces, but surely not the exquisite wrought iron gates that so enhanced some of the parks, let alone the hundreds of public seats. These seats, with their entrancing patterns of cast iron and sturdy wooden slats, had withstood the vandals and weather for sometimes a hundred years, and the cost of continually replacing them with austerity models that were broken within a few years must, since the war, have cost the country a fortune. Even at the time there were letters of indignation to the press, and in the end appeals were allowed so as to save what was left of outstanding beauty. Worst of all, much of the scrap was never used and lay abandoned and rusting until well into the fifties. Still, it's an ill wind, as they say, and at least couples could make love in the gentle darkness of our open parks, rather than knee-trembling against some wall.

Aside from metal, the other great drive was for paper, and as early as 1940 shopkeepers were forbidden to wrap anything unless it was essential. From then on, paper bags were smoothed flat and kept for re-use, as were letters that were written on one side only, the next recipient enjoying a guilty read of somebody else's correspondence; and lavatory paper became so scarce that any odd bits of paper were pressed into service, my uncle complaining that his "sit-upon" was being lacerated by the knife-edged sheets of Aunt Grace's *Tatler*. "Besides, it can hardly be decent to wipe one's parts with a photograph of the Princess

Royal!" Yet another drawback was that what had once taken a minute now stretched into as many as twenty, as users were caught by some article and were driven to hunting through the scraps to read how it ended. When leaving home, many took their own paper with them, for public lavatories never had any, though they continued to charge a penny. Even posters featuring Winston Churchill were ripped off the walls, and the VD notices had to be mounted in stout frames and protected by glass.

With so much paper recycled, newspapers and books took on the hue of the National Loaf: a greyish buff colour, and publishers had great difficulty in obtaining even this. Not that there was any cutback in the posters which continued their remorseless messages: "Your salvaged paper will make bomb containers and anti-aircraft ammo". "Needed: 1 ton of waste paper per 10,000 people a week. Mr Brown's newspaper helps to make the smoke flare for a lifeboat, roof of an ambulance, stiffeners for collars, boots for Russia", who, having been invaded by Hitler, had now teamed up with us. And how extraordinary that such a luxury as stiffeners had not gone the way of the paper clip!

To give some idea of the success of the salvage campaign: by 1944, housewives alone had collected well over a million tons of waste paper, ditto metal; nearly 9,000 tons of rags; over 25½ tons of rubber, nearly 44,000 tons of bones, and thousands of tons of kitchen waste.

However, salvage was only one part of the nation's savings, for we were all exhorted to save money in order to pay for the war, and the Savings Movement which had begun in two rooms in the First World War grew to 600,000 voluntary workers. Backed up by an efficient organization, they preached the gospel of giving by cutting back on personal spending, while the National Savings Committee organized special weeks devoted to saving for separate causes. First there was War Weapons Week, then Warship Week, and the even more successful Wings For Victory Week, and so on and so on. It seems incredible, but in a country where a week's pay could be as little as £3 a week, the village of Weston Turvill raised the magnificent sum of £14 a head, which in contemporary terms of someone earning £200 a week, would be over £900 pounds per person.

Looking back, I can hardly remember any of these drives, for one campaign merged into another until, without noticing, they became part of the background of my life. And, what's more, are a part of it to this day, for I cannot bear to waste food, continually switch off lights, and have been known to boil up left-over bits of soaps, pour the mess into a dish to set, and tip the sludge-coloured result into the soap dish. Top that if you can!

CHAPTER
TWELVE

Entertainment

News Item: 11 November 1939: The village of Pettigo, population 346, spans the border of British Ulster and foreign and neutral Eire. In belligerent Pettigo, blackout is strictly enforced, everyone carries a gas mask, and there is a war tax on whisky. In neutral Pettigo, lights blaze, gas masks are unknown, and thanks be to the Lord there's no tax on the whiskey. A photographer is setting up his equipment when a policeman stops him. "You can't take pictures here, move over to the right a bit and get into neutral territory!"

If anything demonstrates the absurdity of war, surely this is it, though I find it particularly cheering that even at the time the situation was seen as such, rather than a very real source of danger. But then the greater the tension, the more likely it was to generate its own destruction in laughter.

On 1 September 1939, and with two days of peace still to go, I would have thought that the government had more pressing priorities than to shut down all places of entertainment; and though it justified this by the very proper concern that they'd be death-traps in the anticipated bombing, I've a sneaking suspicion that in order to enforce discipline, it saw that the last thing it needed was to be sent up rotten! And it would have been, if only on details, for if the British have a compulsion, it is to prick the balloon of too much officialdom.

Unable to find light relief in the theatre, variety hall, cinema, football ground, dog track or concert hall, the public turned to its only sources of entertainment aside from the gramophone: newspapers and the radio. Unfortunately, both these outlets had become conduits for endless, depressing news and government instruction. Not that the public wasn't avid to know what was happening and what to do, but it hardly needed the cutting of such jolly items as gossip in the newspapers, nor the funereal music that interspersed the voice of authority on the air. Something had to give, and very sensibly it was the governments, who re-opened country cinemas within eight days; while football, greyhound and most racing fixtures followed at the end of October. The last to re-open were the cinemas and theatres in built-up areas, though with earlier performances because of the blackout. However, this helped rather than hindered the audience, who no longer needed a two-hour gap between work and curtain-up in order to change. Indeed, except for rare occasions, evening dress became a thing of the past, and at the beginning of November even dinner and dancing establishments relaxed the rule of "evening dress only". From then on, entertainment became more and more relaxed, or as the Old Guard might have put it, "The rot's set in".

RADIO

Of all branches of the media, it was the BBC that suffered the greatest upheavals. Television was shut down for the duration; and aside from radio departments that had to remain in London such as News, Talks and the vastly extended Overseas Service, much of it was scattered to the winds. Now it's one thing to enjoy listening to radio, but it is quite another to have chunks of it plonked down in your midst. Clifton, that most respectable of all Bristol's residential areas, shivered in its sensible shoes when confronted by the vulgarity of the Variety Department. According to the magazine *Illustrated*: "A blush mantled the delicate cheek of Whiteladies Road, as Bristol folk saw the strange creatures of the BBC roaming the streets . . . Then they saw, they said, Bohemian behaviour, they saw atrociously-coloured shirts and corduroy trousers. These people, they said, were conceited and took possession of the place in a completely unbearable manner!" Luckily, and like so many other wartime innovations, Bristol not only learnt to live with the BBC, but even took a pride in it. Indeed, I've often wondered if the present success of the Bristol nature programmes, in which they manage to record such shy animals as the badger, is due in no small part to the BBC's wartime experience of having to observe and adapt to natives who were equally given to bolting for cover.

In the same way, after the brief dominance of music to suit the start of a war, the BBC adapted to the mood of the nation and went all out to entertain, though it had some difficulty in accepting the first broadcasts of Vera Lynn's "Sincerely Yours". Together with diehards at the War Office, the BBC felt that her sentimental lyrics would

128

sap the fighting spirit of our lads in the Services, and would have preferred the rousing thump of military bands. Happily, such was the popularity of the Forces' Sweetheart that the BBC accepted that she did more for civilian and Service morale than any other programme, and we were allowed to wallow in such delicious songs as "We'll Meet Again", "It Had To Be You" and "Be Like The Kettle And Sing".

Once Lord Reith's legacy of giving the listener what was good for it had been breached by popular demand, new and often irreverent programmes flooded the airways: "Garrison Theatre"; "Much Binding In The Marsh"; music links between overseas forces and their families; "Music While You Work"; Ivy Benson and her all-woman band; and the precursors of the Goon Show: *ITMA* — "It's That Man Again" — and "Danger — Men At Work"! Of all the many excellent programmes, undoubtedly it was *ITMA* that shone above all others, and which fulfilled a need far greater than having a good laugh.

At a time when the nation lived under the mad paradox of an all-out war effort that denied the individual freedom in order to defend that freedom, what could be more natural than that the nation sought relief in the equally manic world of *ITMA*? With a surreal script that demonstrated that any system that ignores the individual must contain the seeds of its own destruction, the series gave glorious reassurance of the triumph of mayhem over too much officialdom. No wonder that the listeners took it to their hearts, when it so perfectly reflected their own battle to survive under the thousands of hastily drafted regulations that failed to recognize exceptions, and which spawned so many forms and instructions that could be misconstrued or go missing, that the one ray of comfort was that an occasional cock-up was guaranteed.

Indeed, manic though *ITMA*'s stories were, they were but an enlarged and distorted picture of many a wartime SNAFU*. For, in the country's effort to defeat Herr Schiklgruber — an *ITMA* name if ever I heard one, though actually Hitler's — the instigators of so much legislation regularly mislaid whole units of the Armed Forces, the legion of the lost happily ticking over on the momentum of Standing Orders; experts in the maintenance of harbours were dispatched to the seaside without a harbour in sight; and when a company of the Pioneer Corps indented for "Poles — telegraph", they were hardly surprised to receive fifty indignant soldiers from the Polish Signals. And if you think this undermined our chance of victory, it was also what we were fighting for: the leeway of a nice bit of chaos, in which we could be ourselves! Then, too, *ITMA* gave us catchphrases that were endlessly adaptable. Set in the town of Foaming-At-The-Mouth, its inhabitants punctuated their dialogue with such pearls as: "After you, Cecil. No. After you, Claude"; "Don't forget the diver"; "I don't mind if I do"; and "Can I do you now, Sir?" We flung these phrases at anyone in any situation, and generally made some kind of sense, but happily not to the enemy, who saw no danger in allowing its mouthpiece, William Joyce, to open his broadcasts with the simple statement: "Germany calling, Germany calling". Nothing funny in that, you might think, except that it was said in such a phoney upper-crust accent, that he could have been yet another of *ITMA*'s characters. Immediately, he

---

*A First and Second World War Expression meaning "Situation Normal All Fucked Up".

was christened Lord Haw Haw, and though he sometimes chilled us with accurate details of what was happening here, his choice of facts often sounded ridiculous. "I hear that such-and-such a town is so dissatisfied with its mayor that the council is trying to remove him." And so was Foaming-At-The-Mouth.

As comedy pushed back the frontiers, so did the Drama Department, and even that most staid of departments, Talks. From the day war was declared, radio became so awash with official information and the sacred News, that there was an increasing demand for interpretation. The words "An expert in . . ." launched many new and popular personalities, including the famous four on the "Brains Trust", Professor Joad running neck and neck with the Church as the fountain of all truth, and giving some excuse for his quite appalling conceit. In contrast, J. B. Priestley's *Postcript* programmes, in which he talked about whatever took his fancy, were models of modest good sense, and were justly rewarded with an astonishing twenty million listeners. Even so, the Conservative Party grew so incensed by what it regarded as his dangerously left-wing views that it managed to have his talks removed from home broadcasts, though they were allowed to continue on the North American Service. Not, I would have thought, a continent seething with socialist sympathizers.

Through the news and information service, features, drama and entertainment, the BBC's contribution to the war effort and morale was immeasurable; though its greatest contribution was through the vastly extended Overseas Service. Regularly, millions enslaved by the Axis and Japan risked the death sentence to listen. Ears pressed to radios tuned so low they were almost inaudible, they would wait for the opening bars of Beethoven's Fifth Symphony that heralded the voice of freedom. These broadcasts, to all parts of the world and in myriad languages, gave a full service of news, plays and talks, plus the coded messages that alerted the Underground Resistance Movements to air drops of personnel and equipment, as well as local information smuggled out by agents; and had the added bonus of reminding the enemy that it might have conquered a territory but not its citizens. Even the British became regular listeners to these messages, mesmerized by the nonsense sentences and their deadpan delivery: "Roses do not grow in winter", "Beryl has lost her book", "Elsie walks on Thursday". On and on went the remorseless voice, and we'd imagine the Underground relaying the decoded information to men and women who would then blow up bridges, derail trains, and commit all the other hundreds of acts to disrupt the invaders. Once, I caught the messages by chance and stopped in my tracks, chilled by the sudden realization that what was funny to me was the difference between life and death to so many. And when at last the Allies landed in Europe, it was the voice of the BBC reporters that took us with them. Together we ran up the beaches of Normandy, together we fought across the fields of France, and when the Allies made their triumphant entrance into Paris, we, too, rode with the voices and shouted for joy.

BOOKS AND MAGAZINES

Before pocket-sized radios and tape machines, books were one of the few portable means of entertainment, especially as the recently launched paperback could be squeezed into a pocket or an overstuffed kitbag. With so many living in bleak billets and forced to spend hours travelling in unspeakable discomfort, reading was often the only solace; but what was extraordinary was that it wasn't just escapist fiction and do-it-yourself books that were popular, but books on philosophy, politics, history and a host of subjects that in peacetime had been read only by the comparative few. But then, when lives were controlled and in the smallest detail, it wasn't just a luxury but a necessity for the mind to be able to range where it wished. Besides, if war creates anything, it is questions. Why are we fighting, what led up to it, what is the history of all these allies and enemies, and what are these countries featured in the headlines? Then, too, with everyone talking to everyone else, curiosity was roused beyond the horizon of pre-war interests. Here are eight people in a railway carriage: a farmer, a nurse, a Czech soldier, a housewife, a bank manager, and three members of an ENSA repertory company, and all of them chatting about their lives and how they are coping. By the end of the journey, the bank manager is interested in Middle European history; the nurse, who wanted to be an actress, has made up her mind to read Bernard Shaw's Prefaces; the oldest actress is about to retire and wants to know more about Wiltshire where the farmer lives; and the housewife who has a part-time job and some money of her own for the first time in her life, has been recommended a book on investments by the bank manager. Also, there's been a discussion about the books that some haven't had a chance to read: two are recommended, while others are considered not so hot, but do try and read so-and-so, it's really excellent.

Such was the passion for reading that most public libraries stayed open long hours, second-hand book shops did a roaring trade, and post offices became collection points for books for the Services. Sadly, at the very moment when books were in greatest demand not only did the Chancellor of the Exchequer add extra tax, but paper became so scarce despite its recycling that in 1943 publishers were rationed to only 25 per cent of their pre-war supplies. Only after much protest was it raised to 42 per cent. Of course, the run on paper by the government and information services didn't help, and while the War Office received an unbelievable 25,000 tons *a year*, the entire publishing trade was allocated 5,000 tons less.

And so, like almost everything else, books became scarce, though possibly treasured more because of it. When I was stationed in the wilds of Yorkshire, I started Proust's *Remembrance of Things Past*, which was published in eight volumes, and though it was comparatively easy to find the first three and the last, the others were unobtainable. Every free day I'd hitch to a different town to comb the bookshops for the elusive four volumes. Nobody thought I was odd for doing it, and when at last I found Volume Four there was jubilation in the barrack room, and two of my mates nearly came to blows as to who should borrow it first.

One of the most heartening of wartime phenomena was the increase in literary and poetry magazines. Despite paper rationing and difficulties in distribution, they flourished as never before or since; but then, it was the first time since the

French Revolution that the intellectual made common cause with so-called common man. Writers such as Antony Carson and Julian Maclaren Ross deserted the rarified subjects of the literary essay, and wrote instead about small and often hilarious everyday incidents, and in so doing they and others created such a demand that literary magazines were sold out within hours of distribution, the Services lovingly passing them from hand to hand in the same way as the girlie magazines of today! As for poetry, when passions are high and tragedies come close to breaking the spirit, it is poetry that almost expresses the inexpressible. Besides, it can be learnt and used as a mantra, it's short enough to be read in moments of idleness, it can be copied into love letters, and, above all, it can be read over and over, and often with mounting pleasure.

If I am proud of anything, it was that I was part of the literary scene at the end of the war. Too young and insecure to even think of being a writer, I was a sort — of literary groupie; and oh, the wonderful excitement of it all, for if there is a time when writers are needed, it is in a crisis when they're the guardians of ideals and, above all, of a people's dream for the future. If proof is needed, when governments or minorities try to bully a people into submission, it is the writers who are amongst the first to be persecuted. To this day, the burning of books by the Nazis, or indeed the destruction of books by any group, has the power to scare me far more than acts of violence, for when dissension is smothered, so is progress and our freedom to choose.

LIVE SHOWS

Early in the war, ENSA — the Entertainments National
Service Association — was established to produce and
send shows to the forces in all the theatres of war, as
well as to civilian workers and the larger air raid shelters.
Despite being headed by the theatrical producer Basil Dean,
whose unpopularity was such that one assistant could only
get through the day by sticking pins in his effigy, it was
an instant and continuing success; but then entertainers
will put up with almost anything so as to get the show
on the road. There was much to put up with: crammed
into lorries amidst basic scenery, props, costumes and
sometimes a piano, they travelled for hours and often
through air raids; had to unpack and set up in halls or
huts that might have one light, no water and no stage, and
yet still managed to give not just a performance, but to chat
to the audience afterwards, before packing and leaving for
the next lap of the tour.

The range of ENSA was extraordinary: drama, music,
song, poetry, dance, readings, stand-up comics and variety;
and despite the call-up of many professionals and the dearth
of young men, some of the shows were of a very high
standard. Even the not-so-hot were hugely enjoyed, and
the downright terrible caused so much laughter that they
often achieved their end for the wrong reason. So let's
give thanks to the foot soldiers of ENSA: the middle-aged
chorus girl, the baritone who'd retired in '38, the comic
with flat feet who tap-danced off the stage and slap-bang
into the scenery, and the sweating declaimer of "Desperate
Sam McGrew" who'd had one too many so as to stay
awake. They were all doing their best; and besides, there's

136

something heart-warming about a wobbly soprano whose feet are killing her and who still manages to smile. As well as the artists, some of the bookings were less than perfect. Chamber music destined for an Army Education Unit would end up playing to male recruits who were confined to barracks, and had looked forward to a chorus line of long-legged and jolly blondes. Not that they were allowed to vent their fury, for Service shows were held under the killer gaze of a sergeant, with a row of officers and the CO resplendent in the front seats.

Of all the entertainers, those who took shows to the Front Line were surely the most heroic, somehow yelling their lines above enemy barrage, or struggling across the desert or through the jungle to isolated units who'd been cut off for weeks and sometimes months. And it wasn't just the performances that overjoyed the audience, but news from home, scandals about the stars, and all the other small talk of happier times. And if ever the prejudice that homosexuals are cowards died a death, it was in the many productions of "Soldiers in Skirts" that braved endless danger and for months on end. One moment they'd be dressed in drag kicking up their legs, while the next they'd be risking their lives struggling through a bombardment to reach another engagement. A rule that must have humiliated many was that at the end of a show the cast had to take off their wigs, and I well remember a glamorous brunette who'd received loud wolf whistles, revealing a balding head to shouts of derision.

Aside from the plays by ENSA and the touring companies, theatres in the provinces and London stayed open throughout the war and most of the bombing, and presented such new dramas as *Thunder Rock, Blithe Spirit,*

Flare Path, and *Love in Idleness.* Many of the plays in the smaller experimental theatres dealt with such themes as the post-war world and "What are we fighting for?"; and which, in the middle of a war when the outcome was uncertain, held an emotional charge that guaranteed a good audience. When stationed in Salisbury, a soldier took me to see Priestley's *They Came To A City.* At the time, the chances of either of us being killed was a real possibility, for we were both waiting to be posted overseas, and we listened to the promise of a better life with an absorption out of all proportion to the merits of the play. The next day my friend was sent to France, and I never saw him again. In his only letter, written in the debris of a town flattened by shells, he wrote that one of the memories that kept him sane was the message of that play.

Of all the many excellent theatre companies, the crowning glory was surely the Old Vic Company of 1944. Headed by Ralph Richardson, Laurence Olivier, John Gielgud and Donald Wolfit, their productions heralded a golden age of drama in which actors alternated starring parts with supporting roles, and which set an example for so many companies since. There was an audacity about the Old Vic Productions that has never been matched, and in which the audience played no small part. Tempered by adversity and the dawning hope of victory, its intense appreciation leaping back and forth across the footlights to feed a cast who then returned it tenfold: an electric charge that was as magical as it was unique.

FILMS

During the 1930s when Britain and the United States suffered massive unemployment, many of the most popular films were escapist. It was the decade when wit, the triumph of the Little Man, and musicals of bewildering luxury reached their zenith; and though Hollywood dominated the English-speaking market, Britain matched it with a few outstanding films of its own, as well as many more that were quite terrible. Still, at least our film industry was *guaranteed* a percentage of the home market by law, so that when war was declared, we had the studios, equipment and technicians to be able to make our own films showing our own viewpoint. Not that Hollywood didn't try and do it for us. *Mrs Miniver* was the story of an "ordinary" British housewife and her family during Our Darkest Days, though few would have thought it from the costumes and sets. Our heroine, in the shape of the perfectly spoken Greer Garson, wafted about in false eyelashes and sheer stockings, her olde worlde house festooned with American "drapes" frilled like a pair of can-can bloomers, and which would have used up more than a year's clothing coupons. Through thick and thin, the parents and their obnoxious children were as perfect as their high purpose, and everyone wept buckets.

In contrast, our own war films became increasingly realistic, and in 1941 overtook Hollywood at the British box office. Even so, many still retained the clichés of the comic Cockney who died heroically in the final reel, the little women who waited with a trembling smile, and the star who spoke in an impeccable accent while portraying a stoker. It is these clichés that so date the films today, in contrast to the documentaries which remain as impressive as when they were first shown. Such films as *Fires Were Started,* *Target For Tonight,* and the exemplary *Desert Victory,* shot during the battle of El Alamein in North Africa, and in which five cameramen out of twenty were killed or badly injured, still stand with the best documentaries ever made.

However, it was neither a documentary nor a contemporary drama that shone above all others, but Shakespeare's *Henry V,* directed by and starring Laurence Olivier, in which the lack of realism enhanced rather than diminished the realities of battle. Who will ever forget the initial slow advance of the endless line of soldiers on horseback, the pace quickening imperceptibly until they broke into a gallop of such ferocious excitement that hairs rose on the scalp?

Despite this, if there is one film that will be scorched on my mind for ever, it was a newsreel. I'd gone to a small cinema in Devon that was packed with the Forces and the locals in for market day. Suddenly, enormous on the screen and without prior warning, we moved through scenes of a concentration camp: scrapheaps of bones barely contained by skin; a man clutching a rag, his crouched frame so emaciated that his joints looked like stones; and everywhere the travesty of faces pierced by sunken and unseeing eyes. The only sounds in the stunned darkness were a woman weeping, someone being sick, and the running feet of a soldier as he tore up the aisle.

HOME ENTERTAINMENT

Because of the blackout and the air raids, it became increasingly difficult to go out at night, and people were forced to make their own entertainment. Always the first to see a trend, as early as the autumn of '39 manufacturers were advertising the pleasures of their products. "Buy the Berkeley Superlux armchair for comfortable blackout evenings", "Make extra money during blackout hours with GTL Tool Chest and home repair outfits", "The Complete Home Entertainer — nearly 1,000 ways of entertaining your friends and children. Get together games, fun round the fireside, stunts and jokes, character quizzes, IQ tests, songs, conjuring!", and under the glorious title "Parents, what of the Night?", Rileys recommended their home billiard table. Not to be outdone, Reginald Foort, "England's Greatest Organist", advertised that he could "teach you during the dark evenings at home — for a consideration".

Forced to fall back on their own resources, families rediscovered the pleasure of making their own entertainment, while impromptu get-togethers replaced the formality of pre-war parties.

It's the winter of 1940 in our typical suburban street, and some of the residents are rolling bandages in the First Aid post at the back of the corner shop. While they're chatting about the fuel shortage and how difficult it is to keep warm, it's the good-hearted Smiths who suggest the first get-together. Luckily, the Smiths didn't give away their piano when the Services Comforts Committee came round begging; and the milkman, who's making a stretcher and can fix anything, recommends a tuner, and will slip Mrs Smith extra milk to help out. Not to be outdone, the next

141

day the children excavate three buckets of coal from under the flattened shed in Mrs Robinson's bombed-out garden, so there's a roaring fire for the first time this winter! In fact, our hostess is so warm she's taken off her cardigan, and with her legs painted with diluted gravy browning, and pencil lines up the backs to simulate stockings seams, she's looking almost her pre-war self; while Mr Smith is in charge of the front door, and is switching off the light and lifting the blackout curtain as the guests arrive. Even so, the air raid warden shouts "Put that light out!", but then what can you expect when he's been hanging about to see who's been invited. It's quite a gathering, and because of the rationing everyone's contributing something to the buffet, including a quarter-bottle of whisky from Mrs Wright, and some sheet music from Mrs Summers. Mrs Robertson can't take her eyes off the whisky, remembering how she complained when the poor woman's son entertained a shipmate on that last leave before he was killed at sea. Still, life must go on, she tells herself, and takes over a plate of food to the old woman who's minding Mrs James's baby. When she returns everyone's started eating, and Mrs Wright's already practising a few chords and complaining about the pedals. After supper, the couple from the corner shop insist on doing the washing up, and as it's freezing in the kitchen they put on their coats. Still, it's best to keep busy when worried sick about their son lying in that hospital with his face half burnt. Above their heads, the children are making a terrible racket playing Snakes and Ladders, and thank God they don't feel the cold, for the room's an ice-box.

Across the street, the old woman has turned out the

light and opened her curtains so as to keep an eye on that broken door opposite. She can just hear the singing, and when they start "Keep the Home Fires Burning", she finds herself crying and feels a fool. It's after nine when she sees the guests leaving, and they're shouting about how they'll meet in the pub to plan the street's Salvage Week, though what the world's coming to when respectable women go to a place serving alcoholic beverages is beyond comprehension. Beside her, Mrs James's baby turns in his pram, and it'll be midnight before he's collected, because his mother's on a late shift. As the Air Raid Warden passes, he points his torch with its pinpoint of light, shouting "You all right?", and the old woman raises her hand and nods.

For those in the Services, the pub was often the only place to find old friends. When on leave from the ATS, I'd head for London and the Wheatsheaf in Rathbone Place, sure that I'd find *someone* I knew, and who more than likely was doing the same. Indeed, the pub became a "Missing Persons Bureau", for regulars would leave their addresses, or if they were continually on the move, use it as a poste restante. Nothing has made me angrier than the recent reviews of books about wartime Fitzrovia, which were so disparaging about the emphasis on pubs and drinking. For many of us, it was all that we had.

MUSIC

One of the most imaginative innovations of the war was the Lunch-hour Concert. They were free, people could come and go as they chose, and many of the artists were internationally famous. Started in the National Gallery in London, they soon spread to the major cities, and such was their popularity that they were always packed, people spreading out into the corridor and listening through the open doors. Besides these concerts and those in concert halls, musical groups toured the country, many playing in the factories, and every Forces' camp had its Musical Appreciation Evening, when the most knowledgeable would play records and talk about a work and its composer. I am ashamed to say that the musical education in my Basic Training Camp fell on tone-deaf ears. Our expert was an earnest officer with flat feet, who was bent on demonstrating that our adored Warsaw Concerto wasn't a patch on a work by Rachmaninov. She played us both pieces, turning with a triumphant smile as she asked which one we preferred. To a girl we shouted "Warsaw Concerto". But then for most recruits, good music meant the Big Bands, and we'd hitch miles to hear one, partnering each other as we danced and sang to "Can It Be Wrong?", "Whispering Grass", and "Don't Get Around Much Any More". The only other source of our kind of music was in the NAAFI, where someone would be sure to be hammering out our favourites, and we'd gather round the piano and sing fit to bust. Mind you, the words weren't always the ones published, but our own and far ruder versions; "Don't Get Around Much Any More" becoming "Don't get around you any more"; while "I'll Be Seeing You" turned into "I'll be sueing you, for all those nights of indiscretion far away", and "Mademoiselle From Armentières" had more verses than "Eskimo Nell".

ART

Yet another innovation was the War Artists Advisory Committee that commissioned artists and sculptors to record the nation's war effort, and which had the added bonus of giving what was then a far more vagabond profession the comfort of regular pay. Indeed, I well remember a painter who had never left the confines of Chelsea dancing for joy when he heard that he was to be despatched to the Midlands to paint scenes in a factory making shells. When I pointed out that he had always said that the Industrial Revolution was the worst thing that had ever afflicted the country, I was informed that I must be thinking of somebody else.

This sponsorship by the government produced hundreds of memorable works, including paintings of the war in the sky by Paul Nash; the devastation of the East End of London by Graham Sutherland; and Edward Ardizzone's illustrations of put-upon squaddies, and rumbustious scenes of pub life during the Blitz.

Most of these commissions toured the factories and towns, and were immensely popular, possibly because they portrayed our lives rather than recherché subjects with little meaning for most.

While waiting for my demob, I was popped into Army Education and, because I was keen on painting, found myself lecturing on French Impressionist painters. Instead of the near empty hall I had dreaded, I found myself lecturing in a room packed to the gunnels, for the interest in art had been so stimulated by government policy, exhibitions and a longing for colour and decoration that any lecture was oversubscribed.

SEX

If ever the pleasures of the flesh had a field day, it was during the war. Men and women who had grown up in the thirties, under the gimlet eyes of parents who made sure that the most the young could expect was a goodnight kiss, suddenly found themselves away from home and without a censorious eye in sight. It was a heady freedom and many took full advantage of it.

At that time, the ignorance of most girls was astonishing, some of them not even knowing what happened when making love, or indeed that there was such a thing as an orgasm. Sex was an unmentionable, something that happened on the honeymoon, and according to many "not very nice". Though my mother was advanced for the time and told me the basics, it was in the barrack room that I and most of the others learnt the fascinating details, though not all were necessarily accurate. For instance, you were born with so many orgasms and once you'd used them up, then that was your lot, one of the few experienced recruits announcing that she'd joined the Army because "I reckon I've only got five a year till the Change, so I thought I'd save up by putting myself out of temptation". How wrong she was. Dizzy from the unfolding landscape of pleasure, we'd sail down to the pub and examine the potential talent: five elderly miners, three Bevin boys and four unfit-for-service. Few took advantage of them, but the lessons we'd learnt set us on the road to liberation, and when we did make a choice at least we knew what we were choosing. And it wasn't only the young recruits that discovered pastures new. Twelve years ago I met a sergeant from one of my camps. Now sergeants aren't human, not to a recruit even forty years on, and I was scandalized when she told me — wink-wink — about the German prisoners of war. "Some worked as orderlies," she whispered. "Well, one of their duties was to bring us tea in bed, and what with one thing leading to another, how we ever managed to get on the square, let alone drill you, boggles the mind." Looking back on the rest of the sergeants, it boggles my mind to this day.

Aside from those in the Services and working away from home, many married women were on their own, and the temptation of a vast horde of foreign Servicemen was sometimes too much to resist, especially as men so outnumbered women that even the plainest was in demand. And what a choice there was! Poles who clicked heels and kissed hands; Commonwealth men who were tanned and energetic; French, Dutch, Norwegians, Danes and the rest, with their romantic accents and uniforms; while the American GIs were so well paid that every outing was a celebration, the girlfriends showered with cigarettes and chocolates from the camp shop, plus the longed-for but unobtainable nylon stockings. Sometimes there were strings attached, and as one recruit explained with some bitterness: "It's one before and one after, if you get my meaning." All in all, women were sorely tempted, especially as the blackout could cover a multitude of sins. In that mecca for all troops, Piccadilly Circus, it became impossible to touch the buildings, so padded were they with men on the lookout for a pick-up, and the prostitutes must have had a field day, for never could so much have been paid to so many.

For the respectable woman, there was a plethora of free entertainment including camp dances, Doughnut Dug-outs and Servicemen's clubs. Indeed, the organizers were so desperate to find partners for their lonely lads, that they provided trucks that waited at pick-up points so that guests could be transported to and from their "dates"; while American clubs had official hostesses, who were vetted before being issued with passes. These clubs were for whites only, the black troops taking their girlfriends to a pub or village hop, for at that time there was little British prejudice. In any case, Black GIs were very self-effacing because of their lowly status back home, and many publicans welcomed them more than the noisier and occasionally prejudiced whites. In one incident I witnessed, the publican served beer to a white GI in a glass that had been used by a black. He smashed it on the bar, announcing that no Southerner drank from anything used by a nigger. The publican turned him out, and though such confrontations were rare, there were enough for the American Army to ask the British Government to enforce the same apartheid as then pertained in the States. After some deliberation, Churchill refused to do so, and the American Army enforced its own. Not that this stopped Black GIs taking out British girls, and such was the fury of a few Southern Whites that they formed chapters of the Klu Klux Klan while *still* in Britain, so that when they returned to the States "we'll stop 'em rolling their eyes at our women".

If the above paragraph shocks, it's as well to remember that Servicemen abroad have always been tempted to behave as they would never dare to do at home, and it is to their credit that most behaved well. However, some did not, and our own Forces were no exception. In the East, it was not unknown for a soldier to shove a film star's photograph over the face of a native woman before he raped her.

On the home front, many men deeply resented the foreigner troops who were taking out "our" women, and a current saying was that the GIs were "over-paid, over-sexed and over here"; while in British units overseas, rumours were rife. Some had reason to be worried, for when they returned home it was to find that their wives had left them, or were pregnant or had already borne children by another man.

By the end of the war, illegitimacy had soared, divorce had more than doubled and there was a two-way traffic of foreign brides arriving here, and British brides leaving for overseas. Indeed, there were so many GI brides that the American Army ran courses to prepare our girls for their new life in the States. Even so, one bride I knew was convinced that her marriage would be "Just like the pictures. I'll wear satin housecoats and swansdown slippers, and what's more I'll have a darkie maid in a black dress and a frilly apron". Later she wrote to say that she and her husband were working in a motel, but such is the power of love that not only was she blissfully happy, but ended her letter with the triumphant words: *"I told you it'd be like the pictures!!!"*

CHAPTER
THIRTEEN

Prejudice and Propaganda; Censorship and Subversion

Since the birth of society, the State and the Church have used words to underline their authority, and to keep the populace acquiescent by a natural desire to be, and to be seen to be, good and moral citizens. In troubled times, the State has used words to retain its hold by extolling patriotism, by blaming minorities within for its own shortcomings, and by denigrating every aspect of those outsiders perceived as the enemy. This is propaganda. We are all brainwashed in one way or another, from the moment we can understand, and mostly for the best of reasons; but the freedom to make our own judgement lies in the knowledge of this brainwashing, and adulthood is achieved when, given new facts, we are able to change our opinions.

The war of 1939 was a moral war, in so far as the Allies were fighting a Nazi creed that was both despotic and evil, and which was built on prejudice and a propaganda of small truths and massive lies that denigrated anyone and anything that stood in its way. That democracies were able to ignore this for so long was not because of ignorance, but a combination of fear, their own prejudice and expedience, which governments transformed into "good" diplomacy, sensible compromise and a convenient acceptance of Fascist propaganda despite all evidence to the contrary.

So let's go back to the early thirties and trace the events that led to the compromise of our compassion, our morality and our recognition of tyranny.

My first encounter with the propaganda of prejudice was when, at the age of five, I was sent to a convent because "nuns are kind". While there, darling Sister Anne told me that the Jews had murdered baby Jesus. Later, a man in a black shirt selling newspapers outside our local station promoted his sales by shouting: "British banks taken over by international Jewry." I knew this to be true, because I'd seen a cartoon showing a hook-nosed man surrounded by money, who was grinding a blonde Englishman into the ground.

Britain was not alone in this prejudice, for we shared it with the rest of Europe; just as we shared the fear of Communism, for it was less than twenty years since the Russian Revolution and the founding of the Comintern to spread the Communist creed throughout the world. What more likely than that the millions of unemployed and poorly paid would follow Russia's example and overthrow their governments.

It was this fear for the safety of the state that helped so many countries ignore what was happening in Germany, for at least its new leader was in the forefront of the fight against Communism, driving its followers out or putting them into concentration camps where they could do no harm. And if Hitler interned Jews, Gypsies, Socialists, religious minorities, trade unionists, and sexual "deviants" as well, there was enough prejudice against them for most people to turn a blind eye or even applaud.

In Britain, the Fascist organization of Sir Oswald Mosley's Black Shirts extolled our island's virtues, while blaming our vices on the Communists and an international conspiracy of Jews. They were not alone. In novels, newspapers and cartoons, it was often the Communists and not bad conditions and pay that were behind the strikes by "honest British workers"; and it was the Jews who ground the face of the poor with their money-lending, and who were absentee landlords and plotters against the established Church. They were the "Pakis" of our day, who were called "Yids" and the ironic "chosen people", and when the German Jews fled from the German Nazis, many chose not to notice their persecution.

But the evidence was there for all to see. In 1933, sixty-five concentration camps were opened, and Jews who consorted with non-Jewish Germans were rounded up and punished. In 1934, the Nazis legalized the sterilization of "inferior citizens" — meaning anyone they considered degenerate or sub-normal — and 56,244 were operated upon in that year alone, while Hitler instigated ten commandments of "bodily purity" for choosing a spouse. The following year, Jews lost their citizenship, their jobs and their pensions, and were forbidden from marrying Germans. This emphasis on sexual apartheid was based on the theory of eugenics: racial improvement through judicious mating; and on the Nazi belief that they were a master race whom they termed "Aryan". It was this nonsensical concept that led to the measuring of noses and skulls to determine non-Aryans, sterilization, the control of marriage, the forbidding of divorce if there were children, and the labelling of Jews as "race defilers" and "sub-human"; the definition of Jew being as tenuous as a single Jewish grandparent.

These facts, plus many more, were reported in the media, for the Nazi policy was to publish such acts, both as a warning to their victims, and so that those whom they wished to be rid of would flee the country.

By the mid-thirties, though many were shocked by what was happening, many more had fused Communist and Jew into one conspiracy: both were non-Christian; the begetter of Communism, Marx, was Jewish; and their supposed sexual licence was identical. Obviously, they were nothing but troublemakers, and if Hitler went too far, at least he was doing something about them.

In 1936, a new Fascist leader appeared on the Western scene. In Spain, General Franco led an insurrection of army officers backed by Spanish Fascists, against the *elected* government. Civil war broke out, and in sympathy with Franco's aims of a Fascist state, Germany and Italy sent advisers, equipment, troops, planes and the pilots to fly them. However, instead of aiding an embattled democracy, France and Britain declared a policy of Non-Intervention, while at the same time preventing foreign arms from reaching the elected government, and in so doing assisting Franco. But then, as even Churchill once remarked, the other side were a bunch of Communists. Thus, our fear of Communism far outweighed our abhorrence of the Nazi creed; and though subsequently Russia sent aid to the Spanish government, and there *were* Communists in its ranks, the overwhelming majority were ordinary men and women who were fighting to save their democracy.

They lost, just as the Abyssinians lost when invaded by Fascist Italy.

Throughout this period, a vocal minority in Britain and the rest of the world had recognized the growing power of despotism and protested, but to no avail. Some even fought in the International Brigade on the side of the Spanish government, and were branded as Communist sympathizers rather than champions of democracy. But then prejudice, like the theory of the Aryan race, survives through selection.

In the latter part of the thirties, Germany was so emboldened by the passivity of the outside world that it broke its promises and increased its territory, seizing a bit of land here, some more there, plus the whole of Austria. And still we did nothing, despite Churchill's continuous warnings that if we didn't re-arm, Hitler would continue to plunder the weaker nations. However, he was out of office, whereas the Prime Minister not only believed Hitler's reassurances but gave in to him, returning from a meeting that handed over a democratic Czechoslovakia with the immortal words: "Peace with honour".

This was so transparently not the case that when Germany instigated "incidents" on the Polish border in order to justify yet another invasion, Britain began secret negotiations with the Russians; for if they were our allies, Hitler would hardly risk yet another extension of his territory. It was too late. In August 1939, there came the shock announcement that Russia and *Germany* had signed a pact of Non-Aggression, and with Germany secure from an Eastern invasion, war was inevitable.

So there was Europe with the bizarre result of years of political contortion: a Fascist Germany had negotiated an allegiance with its enemy, Communist Russia, who had rejected a democracy that was equally fearful of its creed. Ideologies had foundered and expediency had failed; while prejudice and propaganda had done much to blind the world to the jaws of evil that can begin with an insignificant snap, and if not stopped, devour all that stands in its path.

Wartime propaganda can be divided into the negative and the positive: suppressing home facts that are detrimental, while denigrating the enemy with both truth and lies; and propagating all that is praiseworthy and in the interests of the country.

For the British propaganda machine, the Russian/German pact had produced one bonus, for though Germany would be its main target because of its threat to us, its work was made easier because the twin enemies of Fascism and Communism were now on the same side.

Often the first indication of a change of attitude is how we refer to people, and even before the outbreak of war, that most correct of institutions, the BBC, sometimes dropped the title of *Herr* Hitler and referred to him as Hitler. The change was not lost on the listeners, for in the formal atmosphere of the thirties, employers were called Mr or Mrs So-and-so, whereas they would call those who were far beneath them by their surname alone. Once war was declared and Hitler became the official enemy, the media was free to call him all manner of names, including the Nazi Frankenstein, the Evil Leader, and Churchill's Herr Schicklgruber, with its inspired combination of his real and ridiculous surname, plus the sarcastic emphasis of a formal prefix.

In the same way, our tabloid press demonstrated a respect that turned to affection by the way it referred to Churchill, for it moved from Mr Winston Churchill, to Winston Churchill, to our Leader, and finally the endearing Winnie. But then, if ever a man was a gift to propaganda, he was it, for his face was the perfect amalgam of the British Bulldog, and the grin of our favourite schoolboy, William Brown; his voice ranged from the thunderous to barely suppressed laughter; his speeches and their rhythm conjured up our literature and history, and gave us back our sorely dented pride; and his wardrobe was a stroke of sheer genius. Not for Churchill the toy soldier uniform of dictatorship that distances the populace, but the crumpled, tobacco-dusted suit of a man who had no need to impress; and which, when the going got tough, was joined by the siren suit, that everyman outfit of the Blitz. As for his headgear! It ranged from a battered homburg to a peaked cap, a fur hat and a sort of stetson. The man was incorrigible. And not just in what he wore. Who else but Churchill would have dared to take the two-fingered and insulting "Up Yours" of the British workman, and simply by turning the fingers around, make it the "V" for Victory sign that would appear in every occupied country as the graffiti of resistance? It certainly denigrated the very same gesture used by the German troops when they swore their allegiance!

But back to name-calling. A universal put-down of one man by another is the undermining of his sexuality, and in times of war it is a classic ploy. Very soon it was said that Hitler was not only syphilitic but impotent, the one presumably leading to the other; and the fact that he was born out of wedlock and at a time when it was shameful gave him the sweeping insult of an impotent syphilitic bastard. Not that it stopped there, for in a song that we sang to the tune of "Colonel Bogey":

> Hitler has only got one ball!
> Goering has two, but very small!
> Himmler has something similar,
> But poor old Goebbels has no balls at all!

An interesting postscript to this song is that years later it leaked out that the Russian autopsy on Hitler's burnt corpse reportedly revealed that he *had* possessed only one testicle. I wonder. Anyway, whatever the truth of it, Allied propagandists were no respecters of physical deformity, and never lost an opportunity of referring to Goebbels's club foot and Stalin's withered arm.

In its turn, the enemy gave Churchill an equal number of nasty characteristics, including the Nazi favourite of Arch Liar, and this despite Hitler's statement in *Mein Kampf* that lying was a legitimate weapon for those in power. In a cartoon entitled "A Nightmare", Churchill dreams he is a gypsy fortune-teller and *must* speak the truth. In another, a charwoman asks her workmate: "Why are you crying, Mabel?" To which Mabel replies: "Churchill promised me a rise!" No doubt there were sexual slurs as well, and they must have blessed the fact that Churchill's father had died of syphilis. Indeed, I remember a cynic remarking that without it *somewhere* in the family, it wasn't possible to become a leader of either side! And this is the weakness of propaganda, for the gap between credibility and going so far it becomes a joke, is but a whisker apart.

Proof of this is that the fountain-head of our propaganda, the Ministry of Information, which should have been expert

in the currying of goodwill, often made itself so unpopular
that it became the butt of many a joke. It was its own worst
enemy, for when it announced that it had 999 employees,
the same numbers that we dialled in an emergency, it was
renamed the Disaster Department. It was also referred to
as the Ministry of Mis-information, and the *Mystery* of
Information, for the most innocuous and morale-boosting
facts were sometimes suppressed. In an early and futile
propaganda campaign, the RAF dropped eighteen million
leaflets on Germany, stating that it was Hitler and not the
ordinary Germans who had started the war, and that they
could never hope to win. Nothing top secret in that, you
might think, but the Ministry refused to release the contents,
and in so doing laid itself open to all kinds of rumour: the
leaflets were full of misprints, it was inaccurate and out
of date, and in one glorious flight of fancy, someone had
muddled the packages and dropped our ration books instead.
Even more disastrous was the impact of the Ministry's first
poster, for by implication it divided the nation by stating:
"*Your* Courage, *Your* Cheerfulness, *Your* Resolution, Will
Bring *Us* Victory." Immediately, the "Your" was perceived
as the public, and the "Us" as the Establishment, and as
one soldier remarked: "We're the bloody squaddies who'll
do the work, and they're the Generals who'll pick up the
spoils."

Later, the posters improved beyond recognition, with
snappy slogans and the magic mixture of succinctness and
humour both in the copy and illustrations, especially those
by the cartoonist Fougasse; though the slogan extolling
closed lips: "Be like Dad — keep Mum" raised a hollow
laugh from wives who now earned their own money,
which was far more than the pittance of the Services'

allowance. This poster was part of two enormously successful campaigns: "Careless Talk Costs Lives" and "Walls Have Ears", with Hitler's head and one enlarged ear eavesdropping from cracks and crevices. In fact, they were so successful that people became obsessed with the fear of hidden spies and Fifth Columnists, and Uncle Charles reduced his usual army bawl to such a low rumble in public that we could never hear a word he said. An equal temptation was to show that you were "in the know", without giving anything away. However, rather than hiding the meaning, it let loose yet another whole raft of rumours. Something as innocuous as "That bit of fluff we're always discussing is back putting herself about in Oxford" might become "Guess — who's up to their usual tricks in the old stamping ground not a hundred miles from where we make cars", and said in such a dramatic whisper that all around would prick up their ears, including the ubiquitous Mr Know-All. Desperate to be in on the act, he might interpret it as: "The place must be Coventry, and her Uncle Tom used to be a telephonist there before he was called up". Equally keen to show he is privy to vital information, Mr Know-All passes his knowledge on to a trusted friend, who is sworn to secrecy but does the same, and in no time at all the sentence ends up as "A secret radio station in Coventry is sending messages to our agents in Europe, and the code name for the boss is Uncle Tom." In the end, this would be reported to the police, and the gossip at the end of the line punished; while the punishment for spreading "alarm and despondency" was a mammoth £50 fine. This did not endear the Ministry of Information to the public, for it was their snooping observers who were employed to listen in on conversations in order to report back on morale. The government must have made a fortune.

Propaganda films suffered the same mixed notices as the posters, especially those promoting recruitment to the Services, for everyone was shown in such a perfect light that they bore little resemblance to reality. For instance, to promote the job of army cook, which to many of us was a contradiction in terms anyway, the cooks were portrayed as slim and attractive women in spotless overalls and headscarves, who *smiled* as they ladled out delicacies to the delighted troops. In fact, the cooks that I knew were lumpy women in stained overalls, who stormed like water buffaloes while stampeding between stove and counter with vast dishes of congealed and unidentified matter; and if we even whispered a single word of complaint, their language could peel the paint at fifty paces. In the canteen at my first camp, a recruit had the temerity to complain about the gnat's pee tea, and was told: "Listen you, be f— thankful it's hot and it's wet", to which our brave but naïve heroine retorted, "So's Burma!" The treatment that she received for the rest of her training beggars description.

Another distortion of the Services was the presentation of women working in "men's" jobs, for propaganda went to sometimes extraordinary lengths to depict these women in a feminine light; and it's a sad corollary to the success of this presentation that television programmes and exhibitions presented now, and which are lovingly researched, unwittingly reinforce this image. To give but one example: in a fiction film made during the war and with the assistance of the MOI, the glamorous ATS driving a convoy truck wore a jacket and skirt for which, in real life, she would have been put on a charge for being improperly dressed. In fact, convoy drivers wore leather jerkins, battledress, trousers, puttees and boots, in which uniform, and unlike their male counterparts, they were forbidden to show themselves in a public place. I was one of these drivers, and will never forget how *I* looked during an horrendous journey through a blizzard in Wales. Our Bedford truck had no windscreen, just two squares of glass for the co-driver and myself, so that the freezing snow blew in from all directions. By the end of the journey, everything, including our eyebrows, balaclavas and tin hats, was coated with snow and ice; the drips from our noses had frozen and cracked when we spoke, as did our lips; and our fingers within our gloves were so cold that when we removed them from the wheel they refused to straighten. Struggling down from the cab with claws rampant, we shuffled forward in a crouched position, boots plonking one in front of the other because our ankles had lost the power to bend. Now at such times as these, there was *always* a passing sergeant, and we were not best pleased when she bellowed: "Well well, I do believe that the ice men finally cometh"! Due to the censorship of obscenities, I dare not repeat our reply.

As there has always been censorship of one kind or another, so its target has changed according to the times. In the more reverent atmosphere of pre-war, the United States film censor forbade any clergymen being portrayed as wicked, even going so far as to rewrite *The Hunchback of Notre Dame*, in which the villainous priest is changed into a Count. Far more difficult to explain, except as a palliative to Hitler, was the banning of the thirties' film *Pastor Hall*, which portrayed Nazi brutality in a concentration camp, and which was reappraised and released as a propaganda film in 1940. This was the same year that a British survey discovered that 17 per cent of those interviewed had agreed with Lord Haw Haw when he said that we were fighting the war for Jews and capitalists. Perhaps it was this that helped to alert the government to the fact that though most of us considered Haw Haw a joke, he might be an insidious influence, if only by reinforcing long-held prejudices. Whatever the reason, in order to dissuade the public from listening to his broadcasts, the Ministry put out the story that not only was he a married man who had run off with a chorus girl, but that he had embezzled the funds of the Fascist organization that he had founded in Britain. Considering he had left our shores some time before, it didn't carry much weight; and as for the chorus girl, given half a chance, many a dyed-in-the-wool patriot would have done the same.

Where the Ministry of Information was both useful and truthful was in the information films. They were very basic, with no music or pompous commentary, just the plain facts of how to put on a gas mask, ways of blacking out windows, and explanations of the hundreds of changes necessitated by shortages and alterations in the law. Far more ambitious were the many memorable documentaries, though like most propaganda films they had a tendency to rely too heavily on sentimentality and the swooning music that accompanies such a viewpoint. In *Christmas Under Fire*, they pulled out all the stops. There were angelic choirboys singing carols; mothers and children in an underground shelter, while a voice comparing their plight to Mary and baby Jesus seeking sanctuary in a stable; and the heroic profile of a civilian awaiting the worst as he set his jaw and gazed into the distance with a rapt expression. Still, it was a marvellous film and copper-bottomed propaganda, for it achieved exactly what it set out to do: garnering support for our cause in the United States.

If truth is the first casualty of war, sometimes it is for that most human of reasons: people need to be cheered up. During the Battle of Britain, when our fighter pilots defended the sky against an enemy set on annihilating our installations, the number of bombers reported "winged" or shot down was very often exaggerated; and as with much else, when something is really scary, we try to diminish it with words, and in this instance, into a game. Single combat between fighter planes was termed a "dog fight"; and the day's losses and gains in planes shot down were announced on the newspaper boards as if they were a cricket score: "Day's play: 181 for 42".

Unfeeling though this sounds, it was in tune with the age of the pilots, for many of them had just left school and the playing-field; just as it was their youth that added the schoolboy slang. A good hit was termed a "wizard prang"; and the slow-witted Constable Plod of the comics popped up in many a guise, becoming Group Captain Plod or, if really disliked, Plod and Sod. Yet another fashion was to use an expression to mean the opposite, so that "Ain't it marvellous" meant it wasn't, and "You've had it" meant you hadn't.

One of the most bizarre U-turns of wartime propaganda came when Communist Russia became our ally after it was invaded by its erstwhile friend, Germany. Immediately, decades of suspicion became love at first sight, Russia being promoted in the newspapers, posters, magazines, newsreels, films and on the radio; and what had once been an evil people now became heroic, and with its leader transformed into our very own Uncle Joe. Up and down the country, towns and villages vied with each other as to which could collect the most money for our brave new ally; Servicemen and women being despatched from Russia to promote their very own "Week", and standing shoulder to shoulder with the Mayor, Town Clerk, Vicar, and the head of the Mothers' Union, with everyone singing "There'll Always Be An England" and pom-pomming to "The Volga Boatman". As for the tableaux that were the culmination of such events, all that could be hoped for was a Russian flavour, and schoolgirls made boleros and skirts out of blackout material, with decorations of rick-rack braid and beads from their mothers' button-boxes. Even so, I doubt that many of the guests recognized them as Russian peasants. Still, it was the thought that mattered, and bookshops sold out of bilingual dictionaries, mayors desperately trying to get their tongues round the Russian for "Welcome to our Ally" and "Friends forever". In no time at all, we learnt to pronounce the names of generals and the towns they were defending; and schools pinned maps of Russia next to the ones of Europe, the prefects being put in charge of the red flags which marked the lines of battle. In the wall magazine at my own school, we featured the progress of the Siege of Stalingrad, and when at long last it was over, we wrote to the children telling them about ourselves, and how we hoped that one day we would meet.

All this must sound extraordinary now, but it seemed perfectly natural at the time, and few of us wondered at our change of attitude and why it had been achieved so easily. Only consider this: how much we shared. Though not invaded, we had suffered it in our imaginations, had prepared ourselves daily for what might happen; had seen in that moment before sleep the desecration of our towns, the shooting of hostages and the murder of our friends.

And however sympathetic our allies from the United States and the Commonwealth were, their cities had not been bombed, night after night and month after month, as had the cities of Britain and Russia. Above all, at last we had contact with another country in the thick of the Western conflict, instead of being cut off by the sinister silence of a conquered Europe. Thus, compared to the common threat, the differences in our ideologies seemed unimportant, and our propaganda judged it so.

Censorship, that complement to propaganda, is always far-reaching in times of conflict, and in the war of '39, there was hardly a subject it did not touch. Because of its brief to protect the population from too much horror, many of the best photographs of the bombing were never published; and though photographs of injured children were released in order to gain us sympathy abroad, to my knowledge all were censored if they were dead.

In a lighter vein, weather reports were suspended once the air raids began, for the information might have assisted the enemy bombers. The result of this was that the population was denied a whole chunk of its favourite subject: the vagaries of the British weather. Suddenly there could be no glorious comparisons nor the chance to boast that compared with the rest of the country, *our* district had suffered greater snow/heat/rain or storms. Indeed, such was the deprivation that a polite pre-war enquiry to someone returning from Scotland became an urgent demand. "So what's the weather north of the border?" we'd fling at a returning Serviceman, who'd enhance his report by an exaggerated account of endlessly sunny days that were hotter than any he'd known. The challenge would then be taken up, and we'd reply in the same vein. "London's been *deluged* with rain for days on end, and I've heard it on good authority that it was the highest rainfall since records began!" The fact that it had been reasonably sunny for Scotland, and that there'd been more rain than usual in London, was not the point. Honour had to be satisfied, and I suspect that more records were broken during the war than at any time before or since.

Again, when someone was posted abroad, the destination was always censored, and a new uniform due to a change in climate was often the only indication. The issue of tropical kit meant that the ship was going south or east of the Mediterranean, so a hint when on embarkation leave might be the remark that moths were going to have a thin time in the kitbag. However, kit was not always an infallible pointer, for there was sometimes a cock-up in supplies or a last-minute change of plan, and the "someone" could end up shivering his socks off in Greenland. Still, a letter home with a reference to a mythical "nice green scarf you made me", could always put matters right. Indeed, getting round the censoring of letters became an art form, the recipient being left with a code of words. For instance, the mention of "yellow" meant North Africa, "grey" meant Iceland, and so on; with "Byron" the code for much action, and "Ruskin" that there wasn't any. Then, too, there were a few codes that were universal: a letter to a girlfriend suggesting that she painted the ceiling meant that the boyfriend was coming home on leave; and "I'm sorry Granny's so ill", when she wasn't, was asking the recipient to send a telegram stating that Granny had died, so that the writer would be granted compassionate leave. This last ploy had to be used sparingly, for one of my army mates killed off so many relatives, that the CO asked if her family had been hit by plague. Leave was not forthcoming.

Always a nation who enjoyed playing with words, we learnt to communicate almost everything. One of my strangest experiences happened just after I'd worked on the planning of a clandestine "drop" in occupied Europe. I was on leave, and trying to find a friend's house during a peasouper fog in Wimbledon. Stumbling along, I knocked into a soldier stationed nearby, and he offered to escort me. Feeling our way forward, we began to chat, and by dint of questions and replies unintelligible to anyone not in the know, I discovered that he had just returned from the very same drop!

Later, I suffered the censorship not only of "destinations unknown", but of what I would be doing once I got there. Posted to a driving course, a company of us were taught the basics of unarmed combat, Morse and, though everyone except me spoke perfect French, Urdu. At the end of our training, we were immunized against such jolly diseases as yellow fever, and it was while standing in line stripped to the buff save for our passion-killers — khaki knickers built on the lines of a barrage balloon — and with medical orderlies plunging needles into us as if we were dartboards, that a corporal popped her head round the door and announced: "Bad luck. The war's over." It was years before I found out that we were destined to be wireless operators behind the lines in French Indo-China, later renamed Vietnam.

However, if censorship was used by the authorities to keep us in ignorance, so we, the underdogs, kept them in ignorance of our subversion. The first lesson learnt in the Services was that when up to no good, always carry a broom. This was because it gave you an air of legitimate purpose if someone saw you crossing open ground to the target of, say, breaking into the Cookhouse, Medical Stores, or the Transport Office. The reason for these ventures was the nicking of food or sanitary towels, which would later be sold in a market; while the acquisition of travel vouchers, which commanded a very high price, meant they could be sold to those who wished to make a clandestine journey while their mates covered for them back at the barracks. Indeed, there was an old army saying that "If it can be moved it can be nicked", and this applied to all ranks, for a very successful nightclub owner founded his fortune when he was in charge of an Army Transport Pool, where he flogged not only petrol but various vehicles. After the war, he used the money he made to buy a barrow and a load of rationed chocolate that he sold as liqueur chocolates, his partner posted on lookout for the police.

Aside from the Transport Pool, the Cookhouse and the Quartermaster's Stores were a potential crock of gold for those who ran them, Services' rations finding their way to local shops and restaurants, while army blankets popped up almost everywhere. Considering how I was forced to sleep in my balaclava, greatcoat and gloves because the issue of blankets was so paltry, I'd still like to get my hands on the perpetuators of *that* nightly misery. Not that the rank and file always suffered from their superiors' subversion. Far from it. Posted to India, a fellow writer was attached to a group of engineers who were setting up a Listening Station near the Burmese border. Having completed the job, he was surprised to see them burning the detailed plans with some ceremony. When asked, they explained: "If we're the only ones who know how it works, we'll hardly be posted to the Front!"

For those who were determined to get out of the Services, a few pretended to be psychologically unstable or downright mad, but this was a long and tedious process, and women had what many considered an easier solution. It was certainly quicker. Under Paragraph 11, a girl was discharged when she was two months pregnant, and one of my mates was so determined that she crept to the men's quarters and shouted "Para. 11" under their windows. She was hauled in within seconds, and later obtained her discharge and an illegal abortion.

Usually, it was a particular job that was hated rather than the Service, so that all that was needed was to develop a mild medical condition that rendered you inefficient. A middle-aged cook could complain that the heat of the kitchen gave her hot flushes; the application of an abrasive around the head, neck and wrists could be diagnosed as an allergy to khaki; while the secret eating of beetroot which turned pee red, could result in a day or two in the relative comfort of the sick bay; and though I haven't tested it, I was told that if you kept a piece of raw potato under the tongue before having your temperature taken, it could notch up a few useful degrees.

Whatever the subversion in the Services, it was carried out with a dedication seldom applied to legitimate work, if only because it was one of the few ways of asserting independence within a depersonalized regime.

In civilian life, subversion by the IRA had begun long before the war, and at the beginning of 1939, bombs exploded in Northumberland, Manchester, Birmingham and London; and in August, nearly fifty people were injured and five killed. And so it went on, the scattered bombings melting into the Blitz. Towards the end of the war, the IRA sought out Servicemen returning from abroad with souvenirs of looted weapons, especially if they were from the Commonwealth, for they'd have difficulty taking them home. Buying and selling generally took place in a pub, and the IRA accumulated an enormous arsenal that was smuggled back to Ireland when peace was declared and travel restrictions lifted.

On a lighter note, the scope for civilian subversion was endless, and lasted until the end of rationing in the fifties. Anything that was short soon appeared on the black market, and by an odd double standard, people who would have been shocked to deal in under-the-counter food were happy to buy clothing coupons; and though it was illegal for a shop to accept them loose instead of in a book, many did. These coupons were either forgeries, or were sold by the poor who couldn't afford to use their whole ration; while many rich women relied on their maids, and would hand over their cast-offs in exchange for a number of coupons.

With the shortage of alcohol, delivery vans were hijacked and their contents sold on the black market; and illegal stills did a roaring trade, despite the government warning that their products could blind. Best of all was if a drinker had a non-drinking friend and could take over their ration from the off-licence, and many a teetotaller was surprised by his wartime popularity. One hilarious story was told to me by my doctor. He had asked a patient for a specimen of her urine, and she had put it in an old whisky bottle. On the way to deliver it, she had visited a department store, and had left the bottle in her basket while trying on a dress. When she picked up the basket, she found that the bottle had been replaced by £3 and a note: "Desperate for something to take to a party!" Indeed, so desperate were some, that they'd buy black market Dexedrine pills that were issued to air crews to keep them awake during long hauls. These were ground to a powder and added to the watered-down beer, and certainly made a party go with a swing.

One of the few anomalies of our rationing was that coffee was not only *not* rationed but easy to find, whereas in Europe it disappeared after the Nazi occupation. It was still unobtainable after the war, and many of the young and broke, myself included, paid for a trip to France with tins of Nescafé. Early in '47, I hitched to Paris with four tins which I sold outside Montparnasse Station, bartering one of the tins for a plait of natural blonde hair. This is the rarest hair in the world, and came from Germany, where blonde plaits had been part of the image of Aryan womanhood. By '47, Germany was so devastated that hair was all that many women had to sell, but few felt guilty about buying it when newspapers were still full of gruesome details of the hair cut from victims in the concentration camps. Later I sold the plait to a hairdresser in London, and lived on the proceeds until I started work at the BBC.

As final comment on prejudice and the "cover-up", that peacetime word for censorship: by the end of the war, Russia, the United States, Europe and Britain were all pals together. We'd defeated the Axis powers, the Nazi war criminals were to be tried at Nuremberg, and right was not only on our side, but had prevailed and would continue to do so. Or would it?

Many of the Nazi war criminals had much expertise and information which could be invaluable to the victors. Von Braun, the inventor of the rockets, had unique knowledge, and a whitewash could be achieved by not investigating his past *too* diligently, especially when he had been on the executive committee of the experimental station at

Norhausen. At that time, and because of deaths due to maltreatment and appalling conditions, the station had a massive turnover of slave labour, and as a warning against insurrection, twelve of them had been hung and left in the workplace for days. Von Braun must have known of it. Just as the Allies knew that he joined the Nazi Party as early as 1937, though he probably said that he was forced to in order to keep his job! At one point after his capture, he and his colleagues were sent to an interrogation centre in Wimbledon, but they refused to play ball with us, and on returning to Germany, the United States offered them a far better deal, which they accepted. But then, almost all the Allies were hell-bent on head-hunting useful Nazis. A German engineer who had used local slave labour in a French factory during the war was bribed back to the very same factory to continue his brilliant work; and the Russians, who had ingested most of Eastern Europe, gave scientists and their families only a few hours' notice and no choice, before transferring them to the homeland and *their* laboratories.

With the recarving of Europe, and so much of it behind the Iron Curtain, Russian Communists were again seen as the Enemy; while in the United States, the FBI set out to purge their own homegrown variety. Luckily for them, quite a number of useful Nazis had been given entry visas, for their original files in the library at Nuremberg had somehow become pristine, and the information that they had gained torturing European Communists and learning their contacts overseas must have been very useful in the FBI's hunt for the enemy within. But then, in times of peace as well as war, expediency is the name of the game, just as prejudice is a moveable asset.

However, if there is one prejudice that persists above all others, it is against races of another colour. In the Far East, the British prosecuted not only Japanese war criminals, but the natives who had continued to work in the civil service during the occupation; yet the Allies never suggested doing the same to those who worked in the European civil service under the Nazis; let alone the French police who had rounded up far more Jews than Germany demanded. And I wonder, would we ever have dropped the atomic bomb on the Germans, even if we'd been at a safe distance; the Nordic Germans who look like you and me, rather than the little yellow men who seemed so alien?

And if you believe that all this is in the distant past, it is not. The phrase that opens this book is that "War throws a long and haunting shadow", and as I write these lines, Parliament is resisting alterations to our law, so as to prosecute possible Nazi war criminals who live here and have British citizenship. Could it be that some of this resistance has to do with our own censorship? I do not know, but when the Channel Islands were liberated from Nazi occupation, some of the Islanders wrote to the Home Office demanding that those who had collaborated be prosecuted. In a recent television programme, a Channel Islander stated that the answers had varied from no reply to a palliative; and though *he* had persisted, the only result had been a *threat*. Whatever the facts, I wonder if our resistance to the trials of Nazis and their collaborators has more to do with our own past rather than the enemy's?

I doubt that we'll ever know.

CHAPTER
FOURTEEN

Aftermath

So what was the dream that had kept us going throughout the final years of the war?

One thing is certain, there had been no dream at the beginning. But then we hadn't "gone to war", but had had it forced upon us so as to stop the German advance; as negative a reason as the Nazis' was positive, for the belief that they were a master race gave legitimacy to *their* dream of conquering "lesser breeds" so as to found a new world order.

Of course, our politicians lost no time in drumming up national fervour with the catch-all phrase "defending our way of life", though it must have had a distinctly hollow ring for the millions who'd suffered during the Depression. Not that anyone protested, for the belief in keeping ourselves to ourselves was so ingrained that it justified not only a policy of non-intervention abroad, but a near blindness to the suffering at home. However, what we *were* acutely aware of was Class, which was taking pride in any nicety that elevated one group above another. In that microcosm of part of our way of life, the suburban street, professionals knew they were superior to clerks, who kept a distance from labourers even when they lived in the next house. In fact, lines of demarcation were so finely drawn that when the breadwinners travelled to work, they separated into first-, second- and third-class carriages on the trains, and to penny-pinch by travelling in a lower class than status allowed was seen as a betrayal.

Then came the war, and the revelation that not only were any differences unimportant, but that if one went down then all were depleted; whereas united, not just the few but everyone gained. This amazing about-face permeated almost every level of society, for even that rarefied hero, the fighter pilot, knew that he was as dependent on the smallest nut in his plane as the worker who made it was dependent on the pilot to defend the factory. Even so, what was extraordinary was how the belief in sharing spread beyond the demands of the war effort.

It was that subversive body, the Services' Education Corps, that gave voice to this gentle revolution, for they spread the word that our future education should no longer be divided into training the masses for factory fodder and servicing their betters, while only élite institutions need teach how to question and command, and what's more with a Latin tag to put the rest in their place! Add to this the teaching that the Arts and the appreciation of them was for all, and the lectures on Current Affairs that unpicked the clichés of our past so as to prove that a brave new world was possible, and the way was prepared for that most idealistic of reasons for fighting a war: a better and fairer life for all.

It is difficult to convey the purpose and the warmth that this dream gave us. All I know is that the image of our future was so real, and the need for it so urgent, that in the first years of peace, the government passed legislation that gave every citizen basic security from the cradle to the grave; and how it was achieved is a miracle or a lesson in misplaced optimism, according to how it is viewed.

Consider this: Britain had fought from the first day of war to the last, had paid the price of continual bombing and destruction, plus near bankruptcy compounded by debt. To keep going, we had paid for raw materials and equipment by signing away trading rights, and by borrowing such a mammoth amount that we were still trying to repay it in the sixties. Above all, the people were exhausted and longed for an end of austerity, and yet they sacrificed luxuries, many necessities, housing and even food, in order to secure the nation's future. Rationing not only continued into the fifties, but was sometimes more stringent than during our darkest days; the import of non-essentials was forbidden, while all our manufactured luxuries were exported; and the rebuilding programme to replace the destruction of countless houses was so limited that many of the homeless were driven to squat in anything with a roof, a cold-water tap and some kind of lavatory.

Against this background of grim making-do was the heartwarming belief that we were laying foundations that would bloom into the glory of equal opportunity with optimum education and health. In a Britain of post-war privation, a National Health Service was launched; the length of compulsory schooling extended and university education made free for all; the unemployed had the right to a weekly benefit; the old had the right to a pension, plus practical help when needed; and a burial allowance gave peace of mind to the dying. None of this sounds miraculous now, but when none of it had existed a decade earlier, and we'd fought a war in the interim, it *was* a miracle.

To paraphrase Dickens: it was the best of times for hope,

and the worst of times for comfort. Indeed, we lived on a low and a high that I've never experienced since. Of course, there were traditionalists and those with vested interests who regarded the passing of the old order with horror; but my friends and I were young, and as adults had known nothing *except* privation, so that the knowledge of what was being achieved justified almost every sacrifice. Besides, we knew that the world was watching our great experiment, and this made us even more determined to succeed.

As for nationalization: much of our industry and public transport had been directed by a wartime government, and to such good effect that it seemed natural to keep and extend it. What we failed to take into account was that much of our workforce had spent years away from the comforts of home, and showed little interest in working extra hours with added responsibility so as to represent their workmates on the executive. As long as they had improved conditions and larger pay packets, the majority were happy to leave decisions to the professionals and a few dedicated trade unionists.

It is a tragic irony that though it was *our* trade unions that advised the Germans on how to organize theirs, it was Germany and not Britain who simplified union structures, and whose workforce were keen to take part in decisions affecting their future. Then, too, in rebuilding much of its industry and all of its unions, Germany had the added advantage of starting from scratch, whereas we built on an outmoded base. Even so, if subsequent British governments had kept their nerve and the policy of stringent economy in order to modernize industry, we could have ended in the happy position of those we'd defeated, who somehow managed to pay enormous reparations and still achieve a healthy economy. And it is surely no coincidence that because Germany and Japan were forbidden to rearm, they now lead the world as models of industrial efficiency.

For women in post-war Britain, who had had the heady taste of financial independence and a fuller life, the restrictions of the New Look fashion were but a foretaste of what was in store. Despite protest, thousands of nurseries closed; many of the wartime jobs yet again were considered unsuitable for women; while those who'd held responsible positions were edged aside in favour of ex-Servicemen. Month after month, the media glorified women's traditional role as wives and mothers, emphasizing how important it was that they helped husbands and sons readjust to civilian life. Not once was it suggested that Servicewomen might need the same support and understanding. Quite the opposite. While war heroes had no difficulty in finding reasonable jobs, not a few being offered seats on company boards where their names appeared on letter headings to the greater glory of firms, heroines of the intelligence service were treated as a peacetime embarrassment and paid off with a hundred pounds. Women who'd lived by their wits in enemy territory withstanding years of danger were forced to find jobs ill-suited to their intelligence, some of them drifting into a twilight world of drink and sex which at least offered an escape from boredom. To my knowledge, two were murdered, and before you think "Serve them right", imagine what it must be like to be trained for, and then hooked, on danger with its bonus of living each second to the hilt; and then to be dumped into a grey world where talent and training are wasted. No wonder that a few sought out the drug with which they'd been trained to live.

I was luckier than most Servicewomen, in that I found a job in which I was fully stretched, though to this day I have the bitter memory of being a passenger in a car that had broken down, and of suggesting that the engine's symptoms showed that there was dirt in the carburettor. The driver chose not to hear me, fetching a mechanic who took half an hour to discover that the the fault was just that. Biting back "I told you so," I kept quiet, for two years of peace had taught me my place. Indeed, the girl who had driven an army lorry would not have recognized the demure woman who prided herself on refusing her husband's offer to help with the washing-up. And if you think I have only myself to blame, just try to resist the propaganda that spumed out of the media with such relentless regularity. Besides, I cared little for self-esteem, for I basked in the reflected glory of my friends in the Arts. Had I but known it, I was to have the unlooked-for honour of being part of an industry that was to flower into the most glorious and unexpected achievement of post-war Britain.

I have a theory that the renaissance of our Arts came about not just because of our change in attitude to them, but from many seemingly unconnected strands. For instance, such disparate factors as teaching methods and the break-up of our Empire. Where schools had taught by rote, they now emphasised reasoned knowledge, meaning learning to think and form opinions. With the dissolution of our Empire, it became increasingly difficult to use it as a dumping ground for eccentric and dissident citizens. For centuries, these non-conformists had been paid to stay away, encouraged into foreign service or to seek their fortune elsewhere; while the destitute were given assisted passages to the under-populated areas in need of labour. However, during the war this was impossible, and when peace came it wasn't much better, for there were fewer opportunities both in Europe and our diminishing possessions, and no one was allowed to leave the country with more than five pounds.

So there was post-war Britain, jam-packed with dissidents, and not only the difficult and eccentric, but some from the Services whose horizons had been broadened by travel and adult education; plus the many young adults who had tasted independence as wartime children, and for whom excitement had become a necessary part of their lives. Few from these groups relished the safety of a boring job because it guaranteed a pension. Instead, many stormed the citadel of higher education, which up to the war had accepted only those who could pay, plus a tiny minority who had gained scholarships and whose families could spare them, so that for the first time, the wanton waste of so many of our brightest was over. It was amongst these graduates, plus others whose restlessness and talent needed an outlet, who now gravitated to the Arts, where the insecurity which put off the more solid members of society was an added frisson for those who thrive on the unexpected.

Yet another strand that helped to create our artistic revolution, was that the Government officially recognized the importance of the Arts by creating its own ministry, and what's more with a budget to sponsor new productions and talent. The first minister, Jenny Lee, was an inspired choice, for she not only possessed the vision, taste and determination to head such a revolution, but was so respected that once she received a spontaneous ovation when visiting the theatre. Not something I can imagine today.

Throughout the years of austerity, the Arts expanded

and gathered strength until, in the mid-fifties, it burst into a new dimension. A voice that had never been heard rent asunder the cosy West End plays, the novels of middle-class morality, and a fashion industry dictated by the rich and the glossier magazines. Instead of taste filtering down from above, an untapped talent rose from below, giving us such plays as *Look Back in Anger* and *A Taste of Honey*, the novels *Room at the Top* and *The Loneliness of the Long Distance Runner*, and the cheeky gaiety of the plastic coat; while on television, plays by Pinter exploded on the screen, and the reverent tone of the historical documentary was buried for ever by the searing realism of *Culloden*.

Within a few years, London replaced Paris as the artistic innovator of Europe, ripples of its energy travelling to the far reaches of the world. And success bred success, for small theatre groups sprang up across the country, all of them hungry for new playwrights and designers; while our film industry jettisoned the old-time hero and heroine, with their classic profiles and cut-glass pronunciation, for characters who were by no means perfect, and who spoke in a variety of accents. As for our music: what began as amateur singers strumming guitars in the newly fashionable coffee bars, ended in the brilliance of the Beatles who swept across and then dominated that mecca of popular song, the United States.

The four Liverpool lads might have been designed to show off our new style: the clean lines of their hairstyle and clothes, their provincial accents, the energy of their music, and the boundless and sometimes surreal imagination of their lyrics. "Eleanor Rigby" could be included in any poetry anthology of that period, the profound compassion for the girl who leaves her face by the door, and the vicar who darns his sock in the night, still startling after all these years.

To say that the new respect for the Arts, and the country's investment in them, paid dividends, is to state the literal truth. Never has such a comparatively modest investment brought such a huge return, for the Arts not only became one of our biggest exports, but attracted much foreign currency through the tourists who began to flock to our shores. But it wasn't just money that Britain reaped, for the Arts filled the vacuum left by our loss of power. Where once we had dictated through gunboat tactics, we now influenced through the heart and the mind. Our songs encircled the world, our plays made up 51 per cent of those performed in the world's theatres, our television programmes were the envy of the world, as was our satire; and in the not-too-distant future, Francis Bacon would be recognized as the world's finest living painter. And let's not forget the Hippies, those mould-breakers who are so denigrated now, but who nevertheless started the movement for wholesome food and an improved environment. No mean achievement.

So hurrah for the legacy of that wartime dream, a better and a fairer life for all, which spread its artistic bounty into the life blood of the people, who then returned it tenfold. As we axe the people's means of expression and discovery, the fringe theatres, the teaching of music and drama in our schools, the budgets of public libraries, and myriad other creative ventures, we not only cut off the seed corn of future earnings abroad, but show an indifference to the quality of life of our poorer citizens, that is as insulting as it is short-sighted.

The dream is dying.

INDEX

ATS (Auxiliary Territorial
  Service), 82, 84, 85-6, 160-1
advertisements, 9-13, 49, 54, 82,
  83, 109, 141
air-raid shelters, 4, 6, 38-9
air-raid wardens, 6-7, 42
air-raids, 34-6, 39
Anderson shelters, 6
anti-Semitism, 103, 151-2
Ardizzone, Edward, 145
armed forces *see* services
art, 145-6
Arts:
  post-war renaissance, 179-82

BBC (British Broadcasting Cor-
  poration), 67, 128-31, 155;
  News, 8-9;
  Overseas Service, 131, 132
barter, 58-9
Beatles, The, 181
Beeching, Dr, 24
Bevin Boys, 69
bicycles, 30
black market, 58, 168, 169
blackout, 6, 12, 25, 27
Blau, Tom, xi
Blitz, 18, 40
bombing, 32-47
books, 133-5
British Restaurants, 63
"Brylcreem Boys", 12

buses, 24, 26-7
Buzz Bombs, 44, 45

cars, 29
Carson, Antony, 135
censorship, 30-1, 39, 45-6, 67,
  161, 165-6
child minders, 99-100
children, 90-103;
  employment, 102;
  evacuation, 93-4, 98, 102;
  pre-war lifestyle, 90-2
Churchill, Winston, 33-4, 44, 81,
  153, 156-7
cinemas, 127
class, 66, 78, 174
clothes, 4-5, 90-1, 109-10, 111-
  17;
  design restrictions, 113;
  duffle coats, 20-1, 115;
  "make do and mend", 113-14,
    115, 116;
  rationing, 112, 113-14;
  siren suits, 4, 110
coal miners, 68-9
coal stocks, 68
communications, 8, 53, 158, 161
communism, 152, 153, 172
concerts, 145
conscription, 66, 81, 86

Dean, Basil, 136

fuel, 68;
petrol, 29
recycling, 118, 120-4
restaurants, 63
Richardson, Ralph, 138
Russia, 163

salvage, 118, 120-4
saving campaigns, 118-24
Savings Movement, 124
scrap-metal drive, 122-3
servants, 11, 78
Services (armed forces):
conscription, 66, 81, 86;
recruits, 72, 85;
women's, 79, 83-8, 160;
Services' Education Corps, 175
sex, 146-9
shelters, air-raid, 3, 6-7, 38-9
shopkeepers, 49, 50
shortages, 6, 17, 58, 67, 118
siren suits, 4, 110
subversion, 168-70
Supply, Ministry of, 120
Surplus Stores, 115
Sutherland, Graham, 145

television, 128
theatres, 127, 138
Trade, Board of, 112, 113,
119
trains, 22-4, 27
transport, 7-8, 22-31;
bicycles, 30;
buses, 24, 26-7;
cars, 29;

trains, 22-4, 27;
tube trains, 24
Transport, Ministry of, 93
tube trains, 24

underground stations, 39
unemployment, 65-7, 177
Utility Label, 120

V1 bombs, 44, 45
V2 rockets, 46
volunteers, 68, 69, 79, 84, 107
Von Braun, Wernher, 171-2

WVS (Women's Voluntary
Services), 34, 79
War Artists Advisory
Committee, 145
war criminals, 171-2, 173
war work *see under* men; women
wardens, air-raid, 6-7, 42
weather:
observers, 18-19;
reports, 166-7;
winters, 15-17, 19-21;
Wilkinson, Gilbert, 82;
winters, 15-17, 19-21
Wolfit, Donald, 138
women, 76-89;
conscription, 81, 86;
prisoners of war, 84-5;
services, 79, 81, 83-8, 176;
status, 77-9, 82-3, 84-5, 115,
176;
volunteers, 79, 84, 107;
war work, 76, 79-82, 84